FIRST 50
THE BEATLES

YOU SHOULD PLAY ON GUITAR

ISBN 978-1-5400-5578-1

HAL•LEONARD®

Contact Us:
Hal Leonard
7777 West Bluemound Road
Milwaukee, WI 53213
Email: info@halleonard.com

Email: info@halleonardeurope.com

In Australia, contact:
Hal Leonard Australia Pty. Ltd.
4 Lentara Court
Cheltenham, Victoria, 3192 Australia
Email: info@halleonard.com.au

CONTENTS

Across the Universe

Words and Music by John Lennon and Paul McCartney

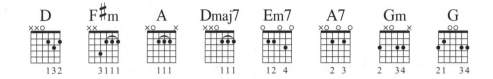

Tune down 1/2 step:
(low to high) E♭-A♭-D♭-G♭-B♭-E♭

Key of D
Intro
Moderately slow

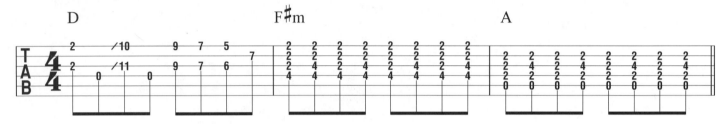

Verse

D	Dmaj7	F♯m

1. Words are flow-ing out like end - less rain | in - to a pa-per cup, they |

Em7		A7

slith-er while they pass, they slip a - way | 5/4 a - cross the u - ni - verse. | 4/4 |

D	Dmaj7	F♯m

4/4 Pools of sor-row, waves of joy are | drift - ing through my o-pened mind, pos - | 2/4 |

𝄋 Chorus

Em7	Gm	D

2/4 sess-ing and ca- 4/4 ress-ing me. || Jai Gu - ru Di | - va. |

A7		

Om. | Noth-ing's gon - na change my world. | |

G	D	A7

Noth-ing's gon - na change my world. | | Noth-ing's gon - na change my world. |

| G   D |
| Noth - ing's gon - na change   my world. |

Verse

| D   Dmaj7   F♯m |
| 2. Im-ag - es   of   bro-ken light   which | dance be-fore   me   like   a mil - lion eyes, |

| Em7   A7 |
| they   call   me   on and   on   a - cross | the   u - ni - verse. |

| D   Dmaj7   F♯m |
| Thoughts me-an - der   like   a rest - less | wind in - side   a   let-ter box,   they |

D.S. al Coda 1

| Em7   A7 |
| tum - ble blind - ly   as   they make their | **5/4** way a - cross   the   un - i - verse. **4/4** |

⊕ **Coda 1**

Verse

| D   Dmaj7   F♯m |
| 3. Sounds of laugh - ter, shades of life   are | ring - ing through my   o-pened ears,   in - **2/4** |

| Em7   Gm   D   Dmaj7 |
| **2/4** cit - ing and in - **4/4** vit - ing me. | Lim-it - less,   un - dy-ing love, which |

D.S. al Coda 2

| F♯m   Em7   A7 |
| shines a - round me like a mil - lion | suns, it calls me on and on   a-cross | the u-ni-verse. |

⊕ **Coda 2**

Outro   *Repeat and fade*

| D |
| Jai   Gu - ru   De | - va. |

5

All My Loving

Words and Music by John Lennon and Paul McCartney

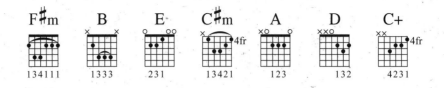

Key of E

 Verse

Moderately

| N.C. | F#m | B | E |

|4/4| 1. Close your eyes ‖: (1., 3.) and I'll kiss | you. to -|mor - row I'll miss|
| | (2.) that I'm kiss |- ing the |lips I am miss-|

| C#m | A | F#m | D |

| you. Re-|mem - ber I'll |al - ways be |true.⟩|
|- ing, and|hope that my |dreams will come|true.⟩|

| B | F#m | B |

| And then |while I'm a - way |I'll write|

| E | C#m | A |

| home ev - 'ry day |and I'll |send all my|

| B | E | 1. N.C. |

| lov - ing to you. | | 2. I'll pre-tend :‖|

2.

Chorus

| N.C. | C#m | C+ |

| All my ‖lov - ing I |will send to you.|

E   C#m

| | All   my | lov - ing   dar -

To Coda ⊕

C+   E   N.C.

| - ling,   I'll   be   true. | | ‖

Guitar Solo

A   E

| | | | | |

D.S. al Coda
(take 2nd ending)

F#m   B   E   N.C.

| | | | 3. Close   your   eyes ‖

⊕ **Coda**

Outro

E   C#m

| | All   my   ‖ lov - ing, | all |

E   C#m

| my   lov - ing, | oo,   all   my | lov - ing |

                       E

| I   will   send   to | you. | ‖

All You Need Is Love

Words and Music by John Lennon and Paul McCartney

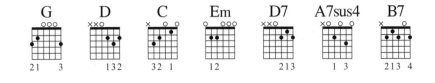

Key of G

Intro

Moderately

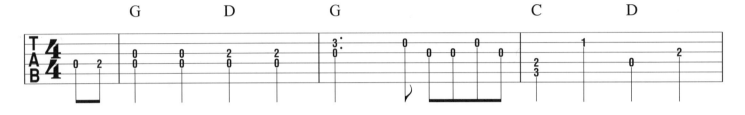

G · · · · · · · · · · · · D · · · · · · · · · · · · G · · · · · · · · · · · · C · · · · · · · · · · · · D

%

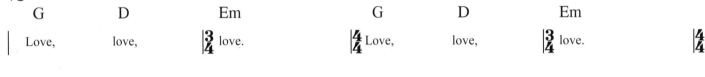

G	D	Em		G	D	Em	
Love,	love,	love.	**3/4**	Love,	love,	love.	**4/4**

To Coda 1 ⊕

D7	G	D		D7		
4/4 Love,	love,	love.			**3/4**	**4/4**

%% **Verse**

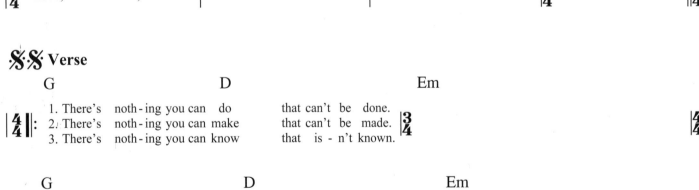

G	D	Em	
4/4 1. There's noth-ing you can do	that can't be done.	**3/4**	**4/4**
2. There's noth-ing you can make	that can't be made.		
3. There's noth-ing you can know	that is-n't known.		

G	D	Em	
4/4 Noth-ing you can sing	that can't be sung.	**3/4**	**4/4**
No one you can save	that can't be saved.		
Noth-ing you can see	that is-n't shown.		

D7	G	D		
4/4 Noth-ing you can say,	but you can learn	how to play the game.	It's	
Noth-ing you can do,	but you can learn	how to be you in time.		
No-where you can be	that is-n't where	you're meant to be.		

D7

| eas - y. | **3/4** | **4/4** : ‖ **4/4**

Chorus

G   A7sus4   D   G   A7sus4   D

| **4/4** All you need is love. | | All you need is love. | |

To Coda 2 ⊕   *D.S. al Coda 1*

G   B7   Em   G   C   D   G

| All you need is love, | love. | Love is all you need. | **2/4** | **4/4** ‖

⊕ **Coda 1**

Chorus

G   A7sus4   D   G   A7sus4   D

| **4/4** All you need is love. | | All you need is love. | |

D.S.S. al Coda 2
(no repeat)

G   B7   Em   G   C   D   G

| All you need is love, | love. | Love is all you need. | **2/4** | **4/4** ‖

⊕ **Coda 2**

Chorus

G   G   A7sus4   D

| **2/4** | **4/4** All you need is love. | *All to-geth-er now.* | |

G   A7sus4   D   G   B7   Em   G

| All you need is love. | *Ev -'ry-bod - y.* | All you need is love, | love. |

Outro   *Repeat and fade*

C   D   G   G

| Love is all you need. | **2/4** Love is all | **4/4** ‖: you need. | Love is all :‖
| | | (Love is all you need.) |

And I Love Her

Words and Music by John Lennon and Paul McCartney

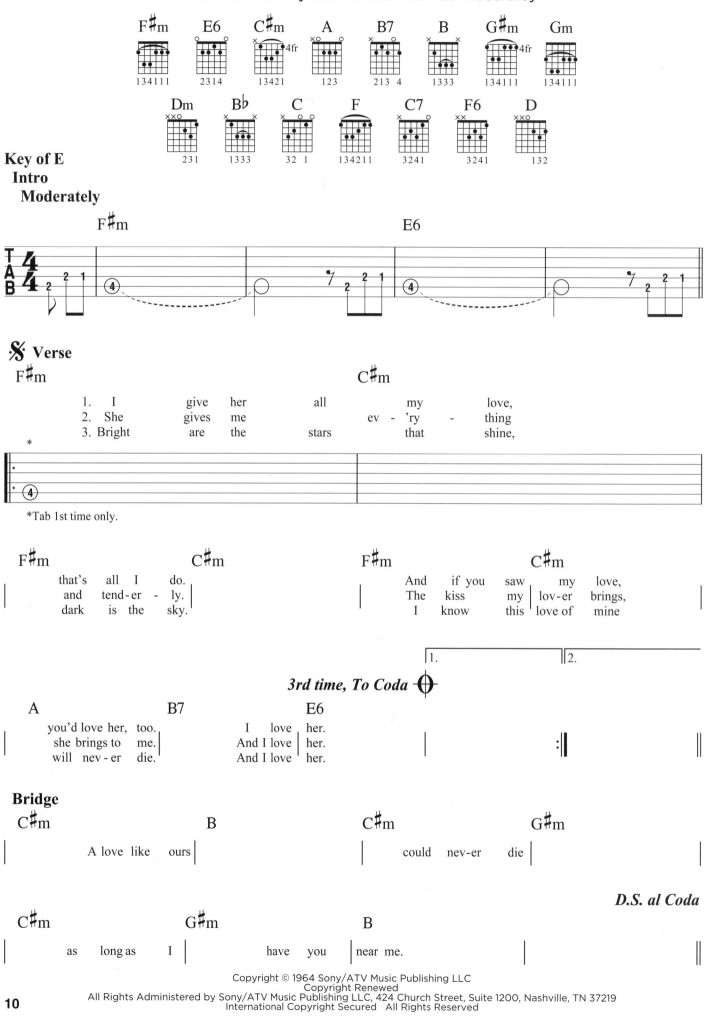

Key of E
Intro
Moderately

Verse

1. I give her all my love,
2. She gives me ev-'ry-thing
3. Bright are the stars that shine,

*Tab 1st time only.

that's all I do.
and tend-er-ly.
dark is the sky.

And if you saw my love,
The kiss my lov-er brings,
I know this love of mine

3rd time, To Coda ⊕

you'd love her, too.
she brings to me.
will nev-er die.

I love her.
And I love her.
And I love her.

Bridge

A love like ours

could nev-er die

D.S. al Coda

as long as I have you near me.

Birthday

Words and Music by John Lennon and Paul McCartney

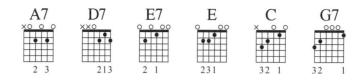

Key of A
Intro
    Moderately fast

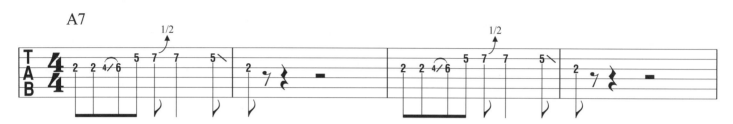

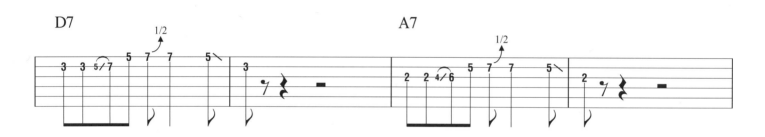

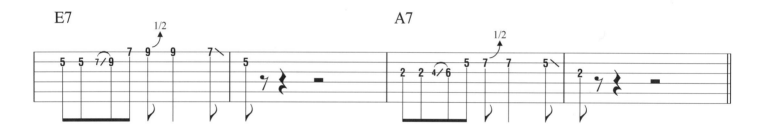

Verse

A7

1. You | say it's your birth - day. | It's | my birth - day too, yeah.

D7   **A7**

They | say it's your birth - day. | We're | gon-na have a good time.

To Coda 2 ⊕

E7   **A7**

I'm | glad it's your birth - day, | Hap-py | birth - day to you.

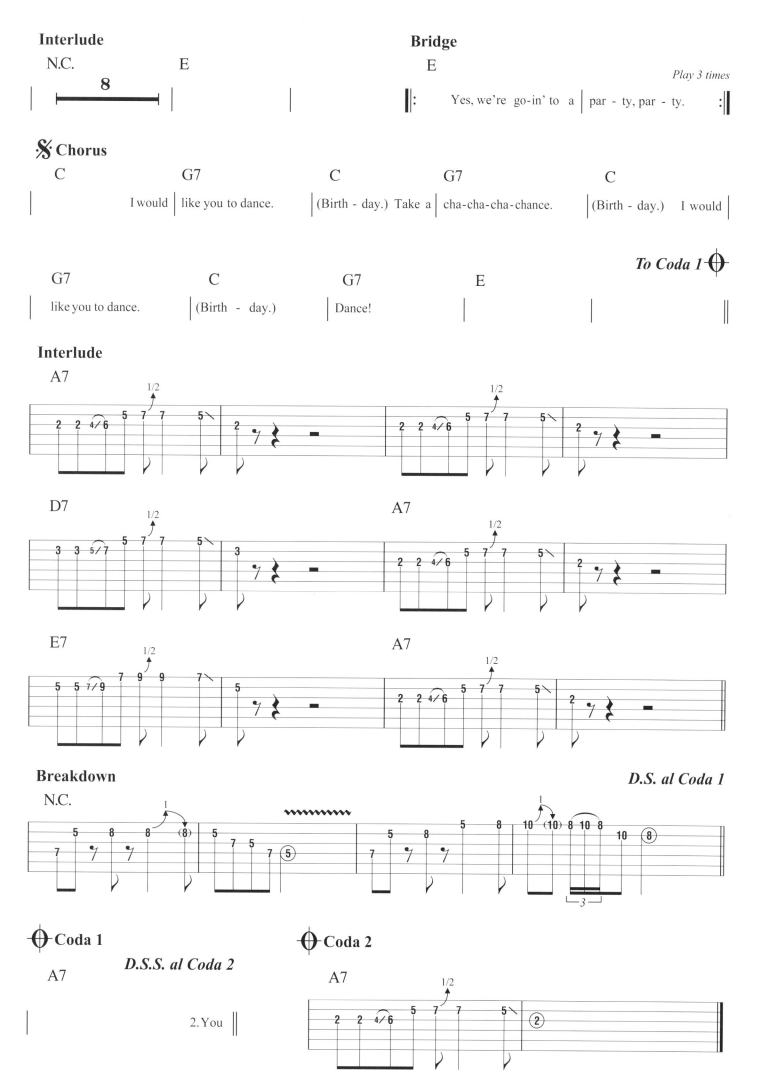

Blackbird

Words and Music by John Lennon and Paul McCartney

G   Am7   G/B   G*   C   A7/C#   D   D#°7   Em

Eb   Cm   A7   D7sus4   F   C/E   Dm   Bb6

Key of G
Intro
Moderately slow

G   Am7   G/B   G*

§ **Verse**

G   Am7   G/B   G*

1., 4. Black - bird   sing-ing in the dead of   night,
2. Black - bird   sing-ing in the dead of   night,
night. 3. *Instrumental*

C   A7/C#   D   D#°7   Em

take   these   bro - ken wings   and learn   to fly.
take   these   sunk - en eyes   and learn   to see.

Eb   D   A7/C#   C

All   your   life,
All   your   life,

Cm   G/B   A7

you were   on   -   ly wait   -   ing   for the   mo -
you were   on   -   ly wait   -   ing   for the   mo -

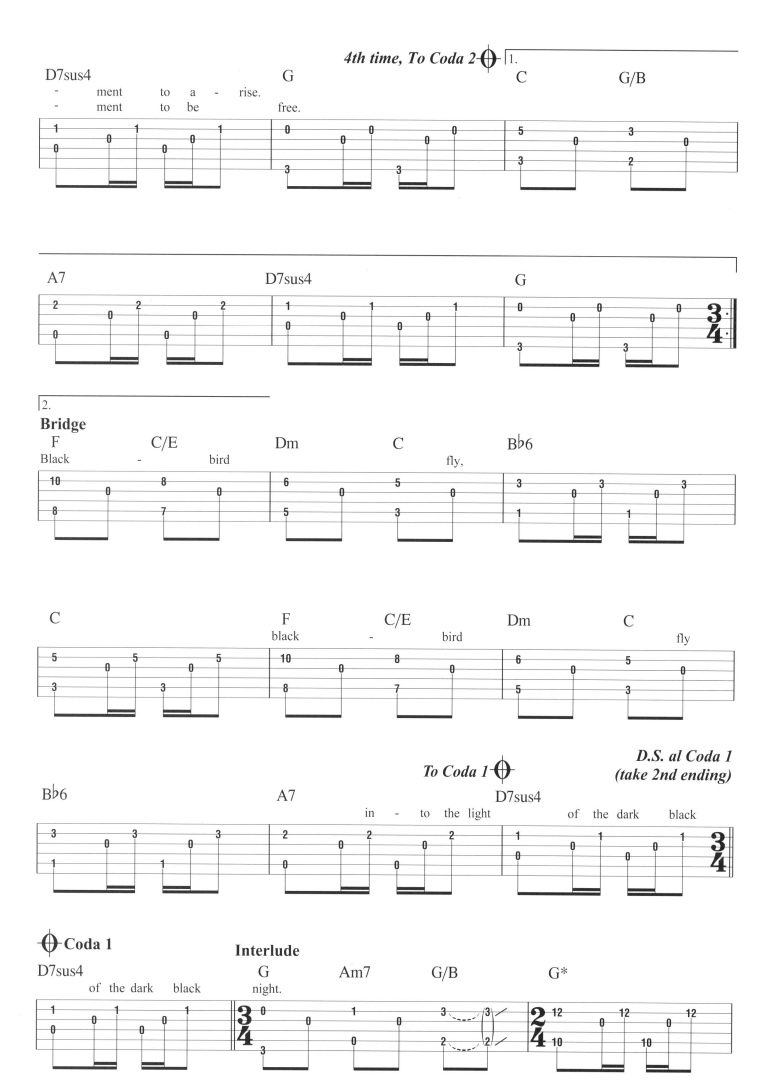

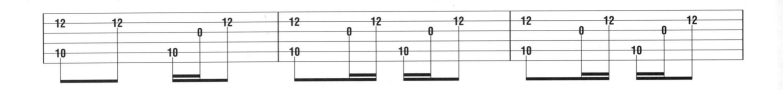

grad. slower

A tempo

G   Am7

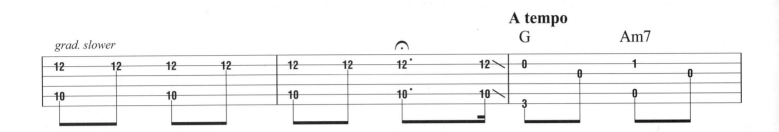

D.S. al Coda 2

G/B   C   G/B   A7   D7sus4

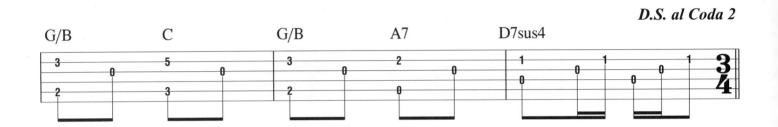

⊕ Coda 2

C   G/B   A7   D7sus4

You were on - ly wait-ing   for this mo - ment   to a - rise.

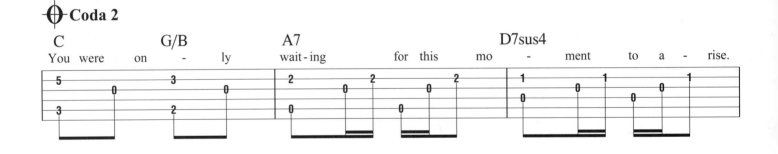

G   C   G/B   A7

You were on - ly wait-ing   for this mo -

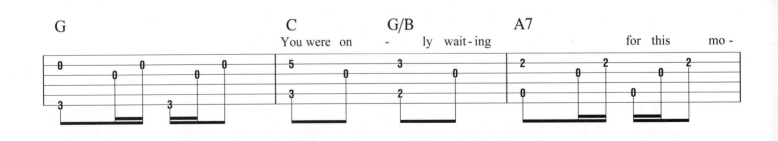

D7sus4   G

- ment   to a - rise.

grad. slower

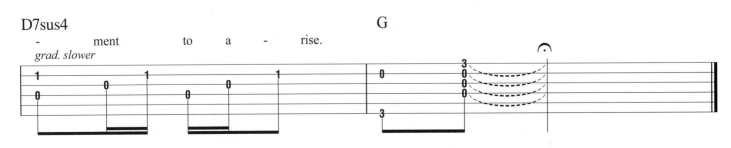

Here Comes the Sun

Words and Music by George Harrison

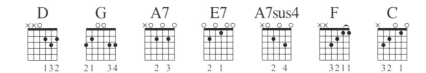

Capo VII

Key of A (Capo Key of D)
 Intro
  Moderately fast

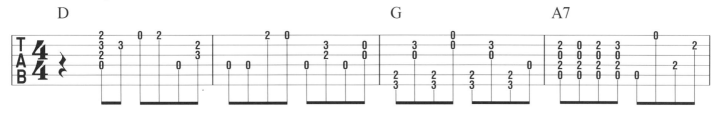

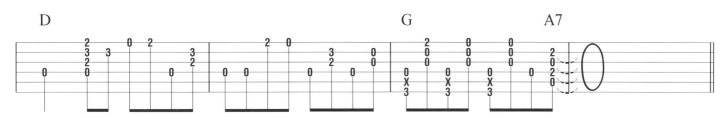

Chorus

D		G	E7
Here comes the sun,	doo,'n' doo, doo,	here comes the sun,	'n' I say

D	N.C.
it's al - right.	

𝄋 Verse

D		G	A7
1. Lit-tle dar-lin',	it's been a long	cold lone - ly win-	ter.
2., 3. *See additional lyrics*			

D		G	A7	A7sus4
Lit-tle dar lin',	if feels like years	since it's been	here.	

Chorus

D
Here comes the sun, doo, 'n' doo, doo, | G here comes the sun, E7 'n' I say

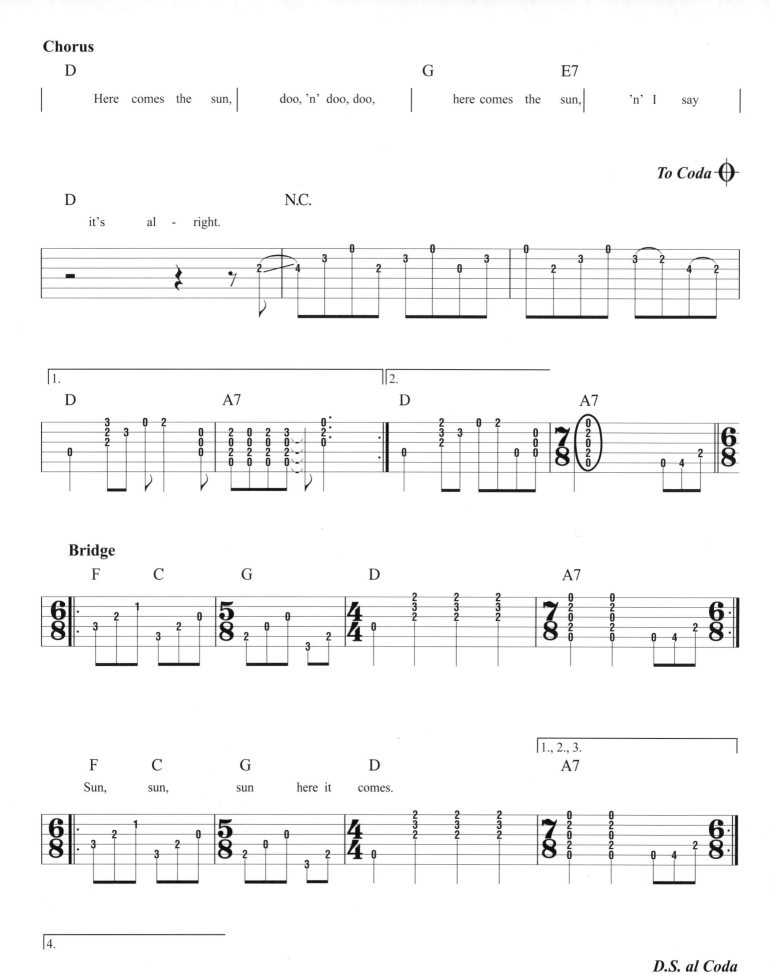

D
it's al - right.

Bridge

F C G D A7

F C G D A7
Sun, sun, sun here it comes.

4.

D.S. al Coda

A7sus4 A7

⊕ Coda

D   G   E7

Here comes the sun,   doo, 'n' doo, doo,   here comes the sun.

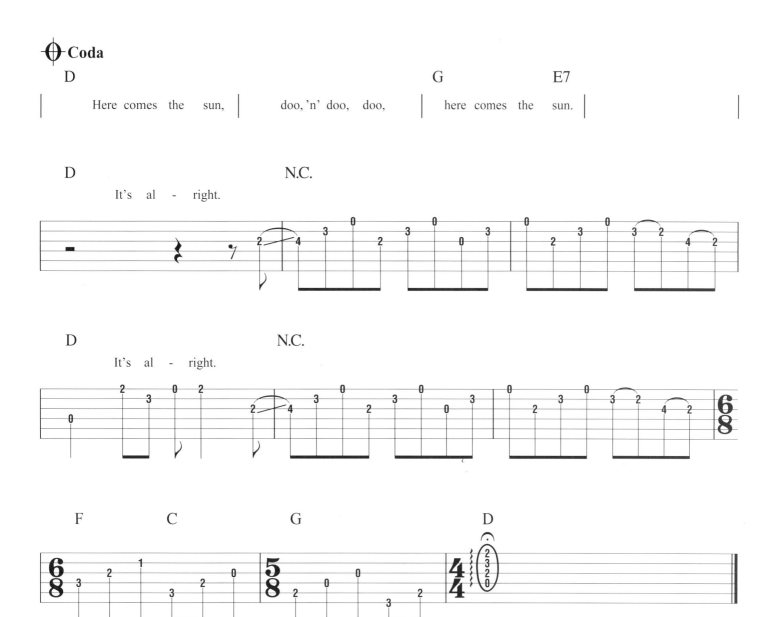

D   N.C.

It's al - right.

D   N.C.

It's al - right.

F   C   G   D

Additional Lyrics

2. Little darling,
   The smile's returning to their faces.
   Little darling,
   It seems like years since it's been here.

3. Little darling,
   I feel the ice is slowly melting.
   Little darling,
   It seems like years since it's been clear.

Can't Buy Me Love

Words and Music by John Lennon and Paul McCartney

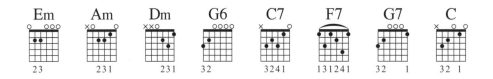

Key of C
Intro
Moderately

N.C. | Em | Am

Can't buy me love, love.

Em | Am | Dm | G6

Can't buy me love. 1. I'll

Verse

C7

buy you a dia - mond ring, my friend, if it makes you feel al - right.
give you all I've got to give, if you say you love me, too.

F7

I'll get you an - y - thing, my friend, if it
I may not have a lot to give, but what I

C7 | G7

makes you feel al - right. 'Cause I don't care too
got, I'll give to you.

F7 N.C. | F7 | 1. C7 | 2. C7

much for mon - ey, mon-ey can't buy me love. 2. I'll Can't buy me love.

Chorus

Em | Am | C7

Ev - 'ry - bod - y tells me so. Can't buy me love.

Come Together

Words and Music by John Lennon and Paul McCartney

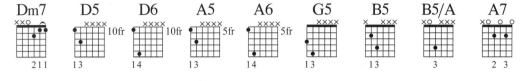

Dm7   D5   D6   A5   A6   G5   B5   B5/A   A7

Key of Dm
Intro
Moderately slow

Dm7

Shoot me.   *Shoot me.*   *Shoot me.*   *Shoot me.*

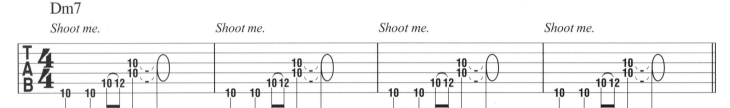

Verse

| D5 | D6 | D5 | D6 | | D5 | D6 | D5 | D6 | | D5 | D6 | D5 | D6 | | D5 | D6 | D5 | D6 |

1. Here come old flat-top, he come | groov-ing up slow-ly, he got | Joo Joo eye-ball, he one | ho - ly rol-ler, he got |

| A5 | A6 | A5 | A6 | | A5 | A6 | A5 | | G5 N.C. |

hair   down | to   his knee. | Got to be a jok-er, he just | do what he please. |

Interlude
w/ Intro Pattern

| Dm7 | | | | |

𝄋 Verse

| D5 | D6 | D5 | D6 | | D5 | D6 | D5 | D6 | | D5 | D6 | D5 | D6 |

2. He wear no shoe-shine, he got | toe - jam foot-ball, he got | mon - key fin - ger, he shoot
3., 4. *See additional lyrics*

| D5 | D6 | D5 | D6 | | A5 | A6 | A5 | A6 | | A5 | A6 | A5 |

Co - ca Co - la, he say, | "I know you, | you know me." |

| G5 | N.C. |

One thing I can tell you is you | got to be free. | Come to-geth - |

Chorus

B5   B5/A   G5   A5 N.C.

- er,   right   now,   o - ver me.

Interlude

Dm7
w/ Intro Pattern

To Coda ⊕

D.S. al Coda
(take 1st ending)

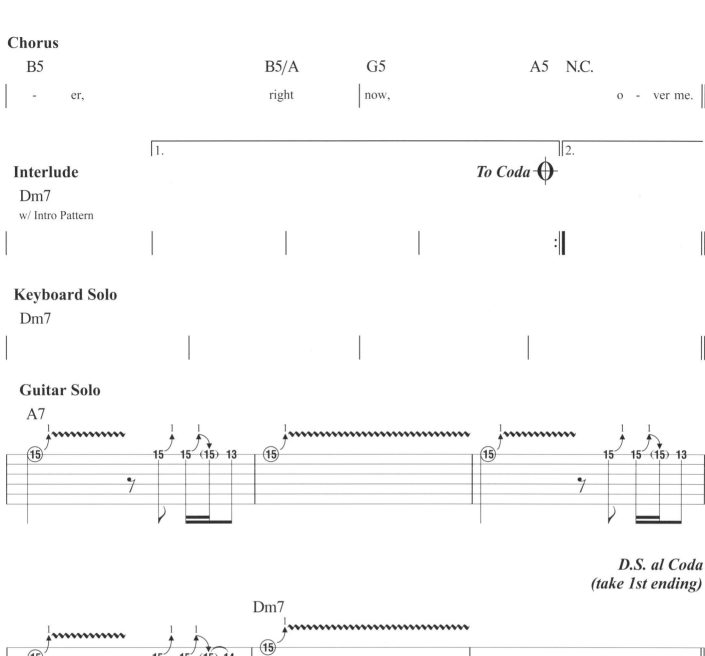

Keyboard Solo

Dm7

Guitar Solo

A7

Dm7

 Coda

Outro

w/ Intro Pattern
Dm7

Repeat and fade

Come to-geth - er.   Yeah!

Additional Lyrics

3. He bad production, he got walrus gumboot,
   He got Ono sideboard, he one spinal cracker.
   He got feet down below his knee,
   Hold you in his armchair you can feel his disease.

4. He roller coaster, he got early warning,
   He got muddy water, he one Mojo filter,
   He say, "One and one and one is three."
   Got to be good looking 'cause he's so hard to see.

Day Tripper

Words and Music by John Lennon and Paul McCartney

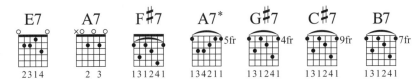

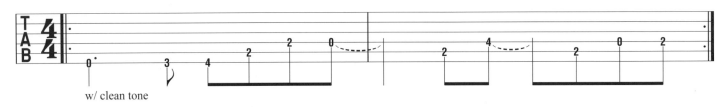

Key of E

Intro

Moderately fast

N.C.(E7)

w/ clean tone

etc.

|: E7 | | :| *Play 3 times*

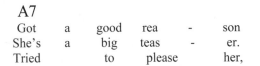**Verse**

w/ Intro riff

E7

1. Got	a	good	rea -	son			for
2. She's	a	big	teas -	er.			
3. Tried	to	please	her,				

tak -	ing	the	eas -	y	way	out.
She	took	me	half	the	way	there.
she	on -	ly	played	one - night	stands.

A7

Got	a	good	rea -	son	for
She's	a	big	teas -	er.	
Tried	to	please	her,		

E7

tak -	ing	the	eas -	y	way	out,	now.	
She	took	me	half	the	way	there,	now.	She was a
she	on -	ly	played	one - night	stands,	now.	

Chorus

F#7

slight P.M. - - - - - - - - - - - -

day | trip - per; | {1., 2. one-way tick - et, yeah.}
{3. Sun-day driv - er, yeah.}

3rd time, To Coda ⊕

A7   G#7   C#7

It took me | so | long   to find out, | and I found |

|1.
w/ Intro riff

B7   N.C.(E7)   E7

out. | | | |

|2.

B7

out.

Bridge

B7

Play 3 times

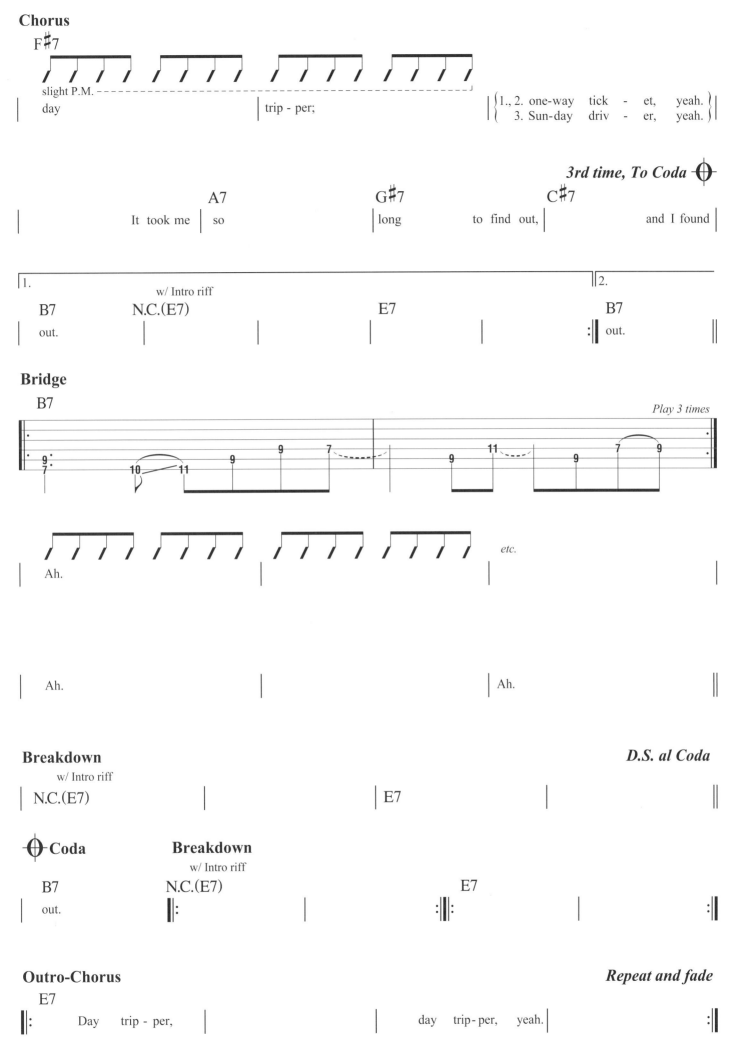

Ah. | | | etc.

Ah. | | Ah. |

Breakdown   ***D.S. al Coda***

w/ Intro riff

N.C.(E7) | | E7 | |

⊕ Coda   Breakdown

w/ Intro riff

B7   N.C.(E7)   E7

out. | | |

Outro-Chorus   ***Repeat and fade***

E7

Day   trip - per, | | day trip-per, yeah. |

Dear Prudence

Words and Music by John Lennon and Paul McCartney

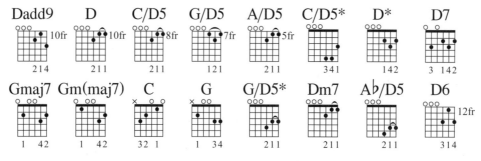

Drop D tuning:
(low to high) D-A-D-G-B-E

Key of D

Intro

Moderately slow

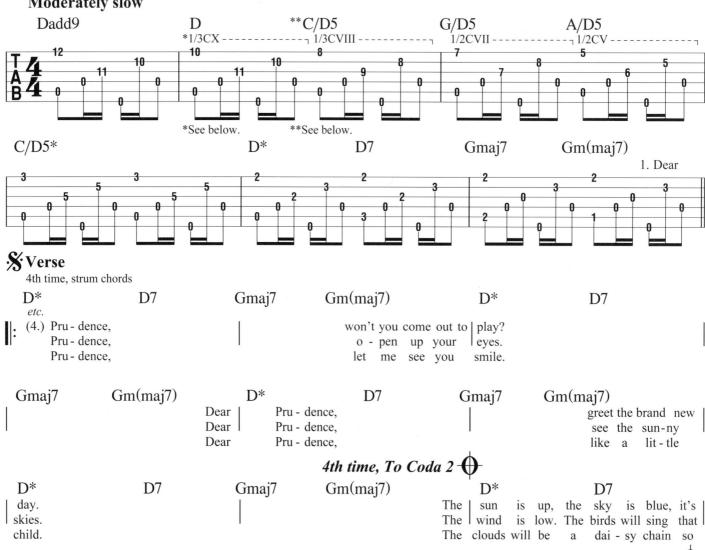

*"C" denotes barre. Fractional prefix indicates which strings are barred (e.g. 1/2 = first 3 strings).
  Roman numeral suffix indicates barred fret.

In this arrangement, chord symbols ending in /D5 denote **polychords: two distinct chords played together, one above the other.

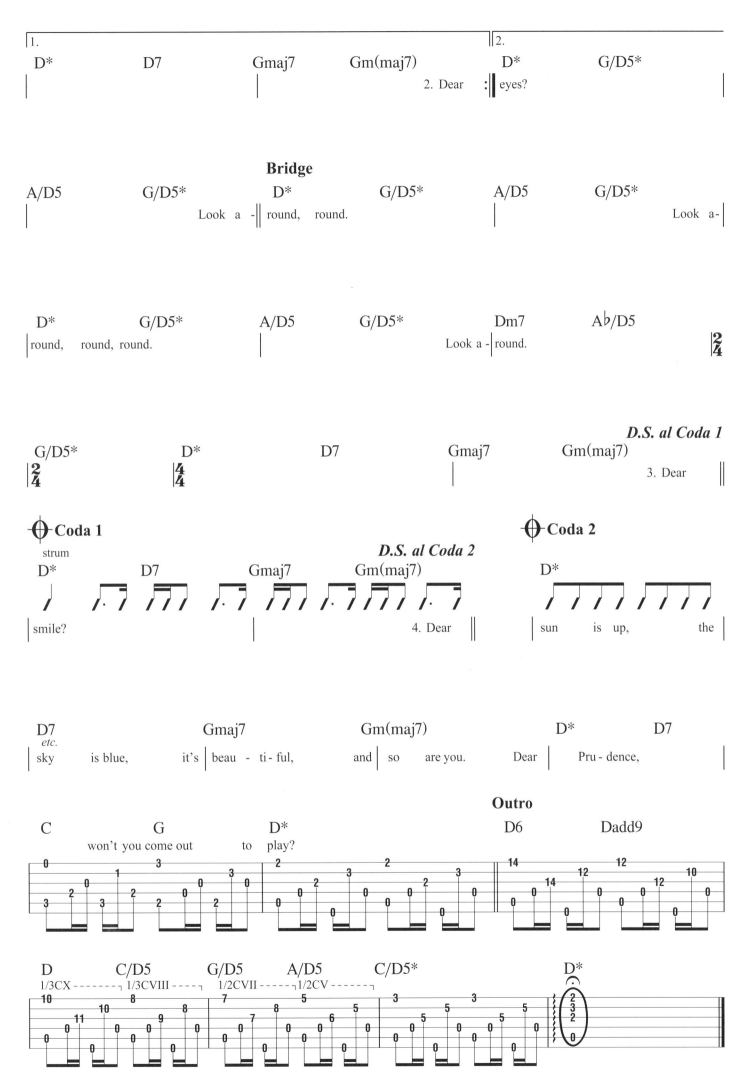

1.

D*   D7   Gmaj7   Gm(maj7)   **2.** D*   G/D5*

2. Dear   eyes?

Bridge

A/D5   G/D5*   D*   G/D5*   A/D5   G/D5*

Look a -round,   round.   Look a-

D*   G/D5*   A/D5   G/D5*   Dm7   A♭/D5

round,   round, round.   Look a -round.   **2/4**

D.S. al Coda 1

G/D5*   D*   D7   Gmaj7   Gm(maj7)

2/4   **4/4**   3. Dear

⊕ Coda 1

strum

D*   D7   Gmaj7   Gm(maj7)

D.S. al Coda 2

smile?   4. Dear

⊕ Coda 2

D*

sun   is up,   the

D7   Gmaj7   Gm(maj7)   D*   D7

etc.

sky   is blue,   it's beau - ti- ful,   and so   are you.   Dear Pru - dence,

Outro

C   G   D*   D6   Dadd9

won't you come out   to   play?

D   C/D5   G/D5   A/D5   C/D5*   D*

1/3CX   1/3CVIII   1/2CVII   1/2CV

27

Don't Let Me Down

Words and Music by John Lennon and Paul McCartney

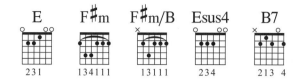

Chorus

F#m — down. | | F#m/B — Don't let me | E — down. |

To Coda ⊕

| F#m — Don't let me | down. | | F#m/B — Don't let me |

E — down. | | I'm in love for the first ‖

Bridge

E — time. | | B7 — Don't you know it's gon - na | last? | |

| It's a love that lasts for - | ev - er, | | it's a love that had no |

D.S. al Coda   ⊕ **Coda**

E — past. | | Don't let me ‖ | E — down. | Esus4   E | ‖

Outro

F#m | | F#m/B   E | | |

F#m | | F#m/B   E | | ‖

Drive My Car

Words and Music by John Lennon and Paul McCartney

Key of D
Intro
Moderately

N.C.

Verse

D7   G7

1. Asked a girl what she want - ed to be,
2. I told that girl that my pros - pects were good,
3. I told that girl I could start right a - way,

D7   G7

she said, "Ba - by, can't you see?
and she said, "Ba - by, that's un - der - stood.
when she said, "Lis - ten, babe, I got some - thing to say.

D7   G7

I wan-na be fa - mous, a star of the screen.   But
Work - ing for pea - nuts is all ver - y fine.   But
I got no car and it's break - ing my heart.   But

A7#9

you can do some - thing in be - tween."
I can show you a bet - ter time."
I've found a driv - er and that's a start."

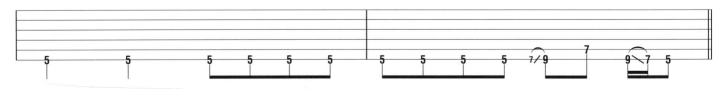

Chorus

Strum

Bm	G7	Bm
Ba - by, you can drive my car.		Yes, I'm gon - na be a star.

To Coda ⊕

G7	Bm	E	A
	Ba - by, you can drive my car,		and may - be I'll love

D	G	1. A	2. A N.C.
you.			Beep, beep, mm, beep, beep, yeah!

Guitar Solo

w/ Verse riff

D7	G7	D7	G7

D7	G7	A7♯9	

Chorus

Bm	G7	Bm	G7
Ba-by, you can drive my car.		Yes, I'm gon-na be a star.	

D.S. al Coda

w/ Chorus riff

Bm	E	A	D	G	A
Ba-by, you can drive my car,	and may-be I'll love	you.			

⊕ **Coda**

Outro   *Repeat and fade*

A N.C.	D	G	A N.C.
Beep, beep, mm, beep, beep, yeah!			Beep, beep, mm, beep, beep, yeah!

Eight Days a Week

Words and Music by John Lennon and Paul McCartney

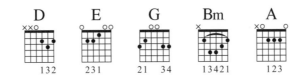

Key of D
Intro
  Moderately

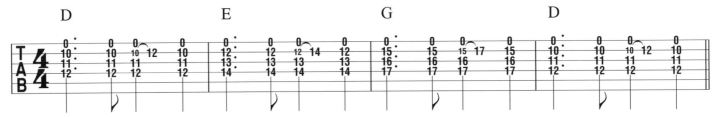

%. **Verse**

    Strum

D	E	G	D
1. Oo, I need your	love, babe.	Guess you know it's true.	
2., 4. Love you ev - 'ry day	girl,	al - ways on my mind.	

	E	G	D
Hope you need my	love, babe,	just like I need you. }	
One thing I can say	girl,	love you all the time. }	

Bm	G	Bm	E
Hold me,	love me.	Hold me,	love me. I

To Coda ⊕

D	E	G	D
ain't got noth-in' but	love, {1., 4. babe,} {2. girl,}	eight days a week.	

Bridge

A		Bm	
Eight days a	week, I	love	you.

E		G	A
Eight days a	week	is not e - nough to	show I care.

Verse

D		E		G		D	

3. Oo, I need your love, babe. Guess you know it's true.

		E		G		D	

Hope you need my love, babe, just like I need you. Oh. Hold

Bm		G		Bm		E	

me, love me. Hold me, love me. I

D		E		G		D	

ain't got noth-in' but love, babe, eight days a week.

Bridge

A   Bm

Eight days a week, I love you.

D.S. al Coda

E   G   A

Eight days a week is not e - nough to show I care.

Coda

G   D   G   D

Eight days a week. Eight days a week.

Outro

D   E   G   D

Eleanor Rigby

Words and Music by John Lennon and Paul McCartney

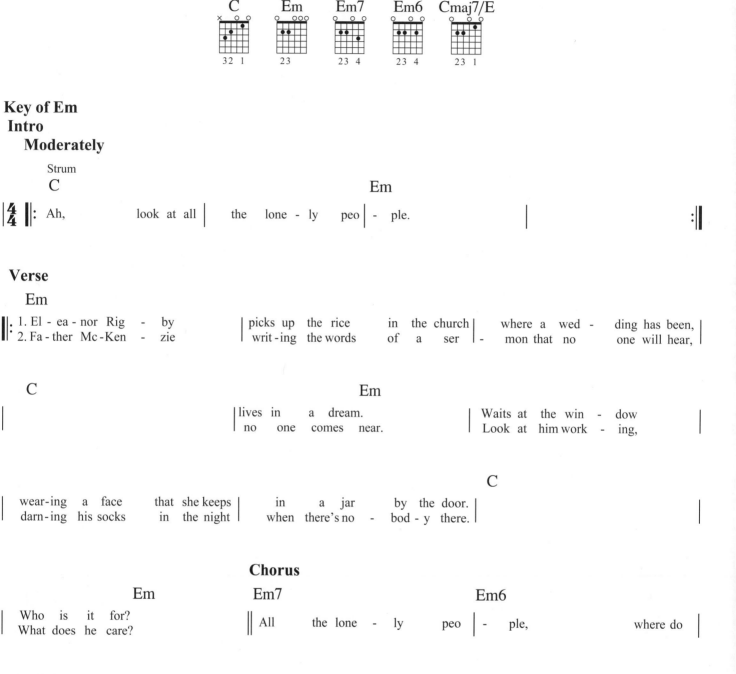

Key of Em
Intro
  Moderately

Strum
C   Em

4/4 : Ah,   look at all | the lone - ly peo | - ple. | :|

Verse

Em

|: 1. El - ea - nor Rig - by | picks up the rice   in the church | where a wed - ding has been,
   2. Fa - ther Mc - Ken - zie | writ - ing the words   of a ser | - mon that no   one will hear,

C   Em

| | lives in   a dream. | Waits at the win - dow |
                               | no   one comes near. | Look at him work - ing,

                                                          C

| wear-ing   a face   that she keeps | in   a jar   by the door. |
| darn-ing   his socks   in the night | when there's no - bod - y there. |

Chorus

        Em   Em7   Em6

| Who is   it   for? || All   the lone - ly peo | - ple,   where do |
| What does he   care?

Cmaj7/E   Em   Em7

| they all   come   from? | | All   the lone - ly peo - |

Em6   Cmaj7/E   Em

| - ple,   where do | they   all   be - long? | :|

Copyright © 1966 Sony/ATV Music Publishing LLC
Copyright Renewed
All Rights Administered by Sony/ATV Music Publishing LLC, 424 Church Street, Suite 1200, Nashville, TN 37219
International Copyright Secured   All Rights Reserved

34

Bridge (Intro)

C   Em

‖: Ah,   look at all | the lone - ly peo | - ple. | :‖

Verse

Em

| 3. El - ea - nor Rig - by | died in the church and was bur | - ied a - long with her name, |

C   Em

| | no - bod - y came. | Fa - ther Mc - Ken - zie |

                                                            C

| wip - ing the dirt from his hands | as he walks from the grave, |

Chorus

Em   Em7   Em6

| no one was saved. ‖ All the lone - ly peo | - ple, where do |

Cmaj7/E   Em   Em7

| they all come from? | | All the lone - ley peo - |

Em6   Cmaj7/E   Em

| - ple, where do | they all be - long? | | ‖

Get Back

Words and Music by John Lennon and Paul McCartney

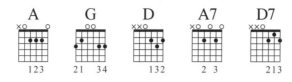

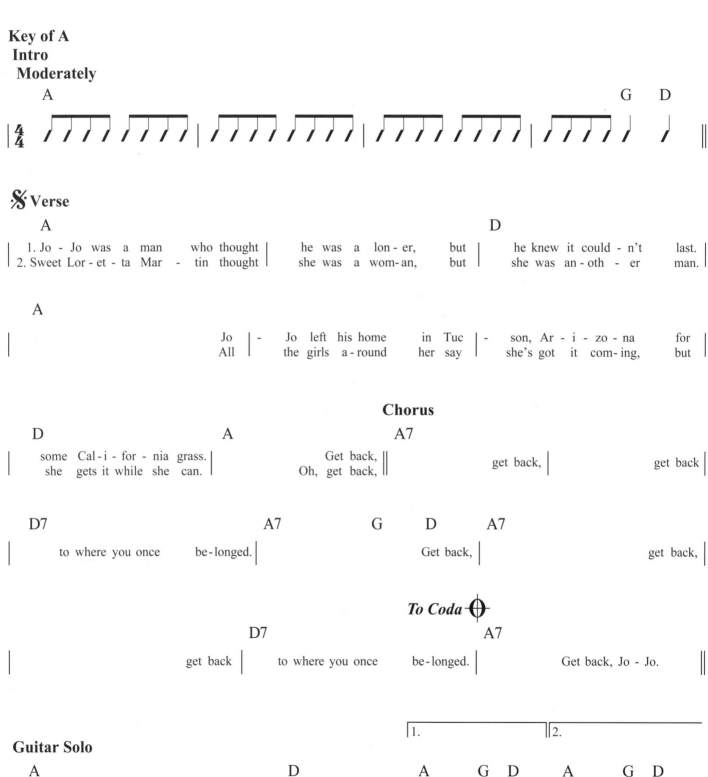

Key of A
Intro
Moderately

Verse

1. Jo - Jo was a man who thought he was a lon - er, but he knew it could - n't last.
2. Sweet Lor - et - ta Mar - tin thought she was a wom-an, but she was an-oth - er man.

Jo |- Jo left his home in Tuc |- son, Ar - i - zo - na for
All | the girls a - round her say | she's got it com-ing, but

Chorus

some Cal - i - for - nia grass. Get back, get back, get back
she gets it while she can. Oh, get back,

to where you once be-longed. Get back, get back,

To Coda

get back to where you once be-longed. Get back, Jo - Jo.

1.   2.

Guitar Solo

Get back,

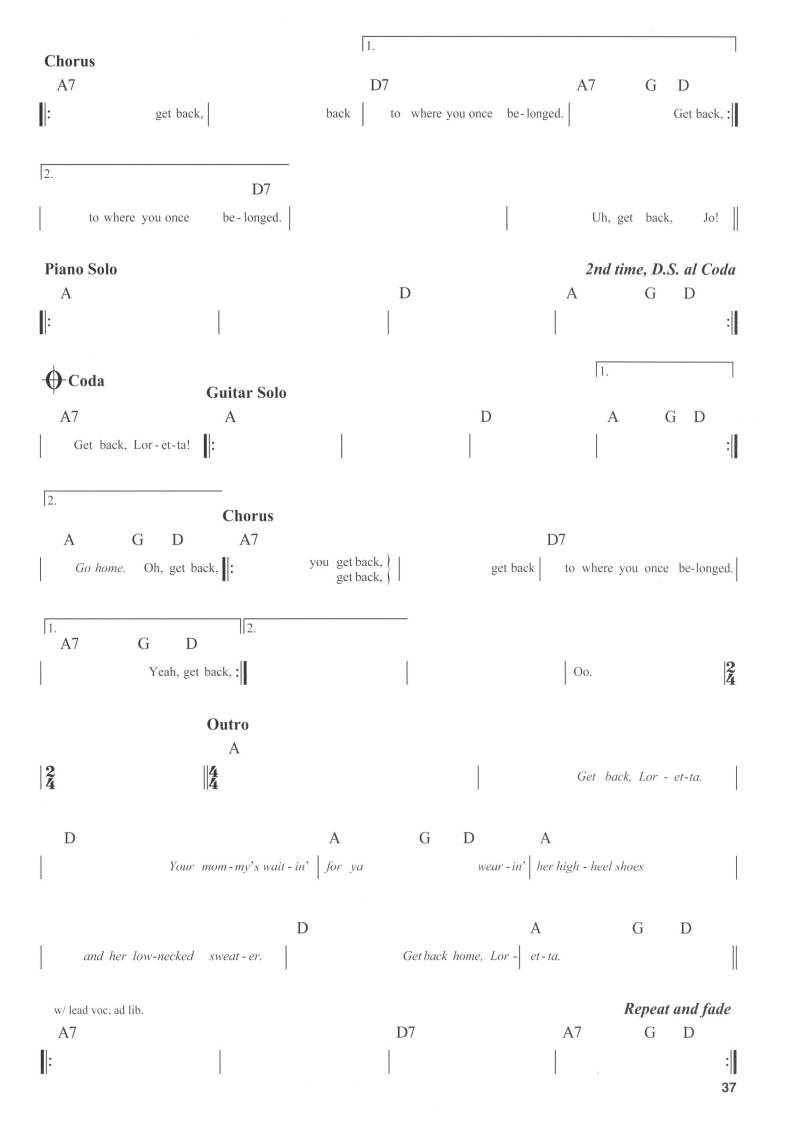

Chorus

A7 get back, | D7 back | to where you once be-longed. | A7 G D Get back,

2. | to where you once be-longed. D7 | | Uh, get back, Jo!

Piano Solo   *2nd time, D.S. al Coda*

A | | D | A G D

Coda   **Guitar Solo**

A7 Get back, Lor-et-ta! | A | D | A G D

2.   **Chorus**

A G D A7 Go home. Oh, get back, | you get back, / get back, | D7 get back | to where you once be-longed. |

1. A7 G D | 2. | | Yeah, get back, | Oo. 2/4

Outro   A

2/4 | 4/4 | | Get back, Lor-et-ta.

D | Your mom-my's wait-in' | for ya A G D A wear-in' | her high-heel shoes |

D | and her low-necked sweat-er. | A G D Get back home, Lor- | et-ta. |

w/ lead voc. ad lib.   *Repeat and fade*

A7 | | D7 | A7 G D

Good Day Sunshine

Words and Music by John Lennon and Paul McCartney

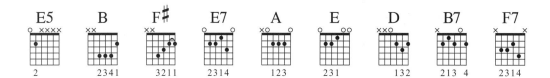

Key of B
Intro
Moderately (♫ = ♩♪)

E5

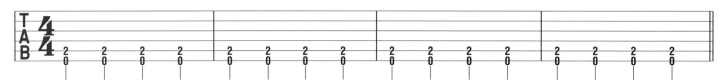

Chorus

Strum

| B | F# | | B | F# |

Good day sun - shine. Good day sun -

E7 N.C.

- shine. Good day sun - shine. 1. I need to

𝄋 Verse

A F# B E

laugh, and when the sun is out, I've got some-thing I can
lie be - neath a shad - y tree. I love her and she's

A F# B

laugh a - bout, I feel good in a spe-cial way.
lov - ing me. She feels good. She knows she's look-ing fine.

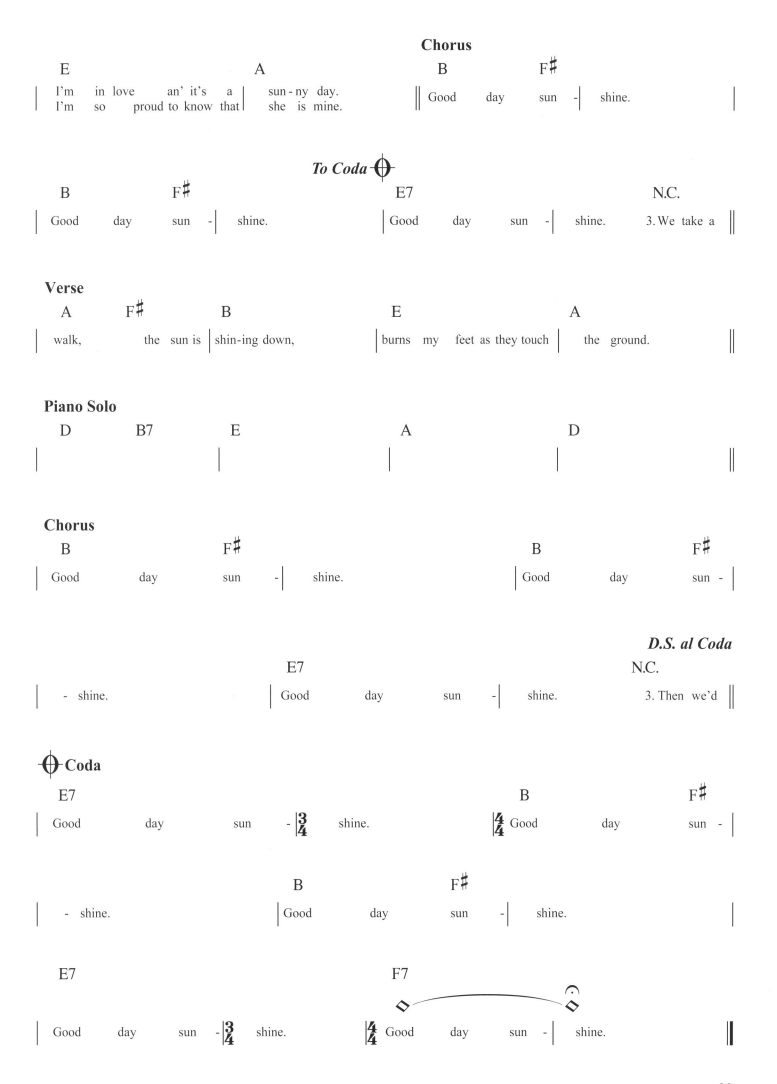

Chorus

E   A   B   F♯

| I'm in love an' it's a | sun - ny day. || Good day sun - | shine. |
| I'm so proud to know that | she is mine. |

To Coda ⊕

B   F♯   E7   N.C.

| Good day sun - | shine. | Good day sun - | shine. 3. We take a ||

Verse

A   F♯   B   E   A

| walk, the sun is | shin-ing down, | burns my feet as they touch | the ground. ||

Piano Solo

D   B7   E   A   D

| | | | ||

Chorus

B   F♯   B   F♯

| Good day sun - | shine. | Good day sun - |

D.S. al Coda

           E7   N.C.

| - shine. | Good day sun - | shine. 3. Then we'd ||

⊕ **Coda**

E7   B   F♯

| Good day sun - **3/4** shine. | **4/4** Good day sun - |

                    B   F♯

| - shine. | Good day sun - | shine. |

E7   F7

| Good day sun - **3/4** shine. | **4/4** Good day sun - | shine. ||

A Hard Day's Night

Words and Music by John Lennon and Paul McCartney

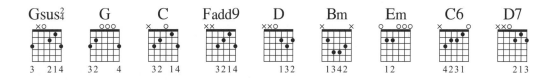

Gsus²₄ G C Fadd9 D Bm Em C6 D7

Key of G

Intro

 Verse

Moderately

Gsus²₄

4/4

1. It's been a ‖: (3., 4.) hard   day's   night, | and I've been
(2.) work   all   day   to get you

G   C   G

Fadd9   G   C   G

work - in'   like a dog. | things.   It's been a | hard   day's   night,
mon - ey   to buy you | And it's | worth it just to hear you say

Fadd9   G

| I should be | sleep - in'   like a log. | But when I ‖
| you're gon - na | give me   ev - 'ry - thing. | So why on

To Coda 1 ⊕
To Coda 2 ⊕

Chorus

C   D   G   C   G

| get home to you,   I find the | things that you do   will make me | feel   al - right. |
| earth should I moan,   'cause when I | get you a - lone   you know I | feel   o - kay. |

|1. |2.

Bridge

Bm   Em

| 2. You know I :‖ | When I'm home, ‖ | ev - 'ry - thing seems to be |

Bm   G   Em

| right. | When I'm home, | feel - ing you hold - ing me |

D.S. al Coda 1   ⊕ **Coda 1**

C6   D7

| tight,   tight, | yeah.   3. It's been a ‖ | Ow! |

Guitar Solo

G   C   G   Fadd9

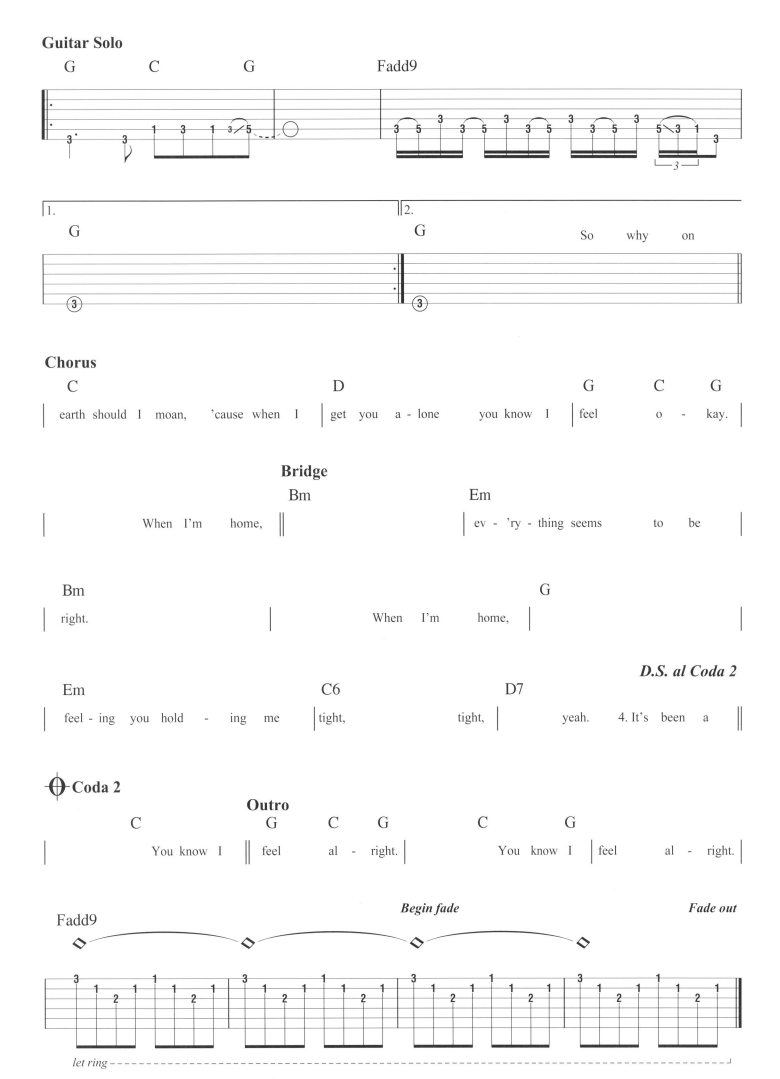

1.
G

2.
G   So   why   on

Chorus

C   D   G   C   G

| earth should I moan,   'cause when I | get you a - lone   you know I | feel   o - kay. |

Bridge

Bm   Em

| When I'm   home, ‖ | ev - 'ry - thing seems   to   be |

Bm   G

| right. | When I'm   home, |

D.S. al Coda 2

Em   C6   D7

| feel - ing you hold - ing me | tight,   tight, | yeah.   4. It's been a ‖

Coda 2

Outro

C   G   C   G   C   G

| You know I ‖ feel   al - right. | You know I | feel   al - right. |

Begin fade   *Fade out*

Fadd9

let ring -

Hello, Goodbye

Words and Music by John Lennon and Paul McCartney

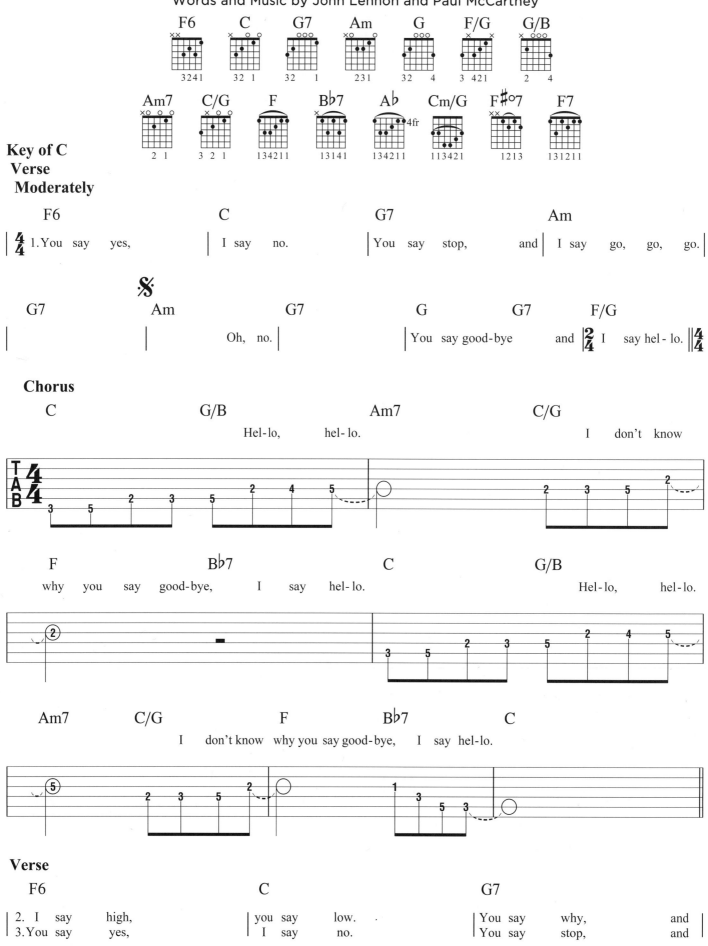

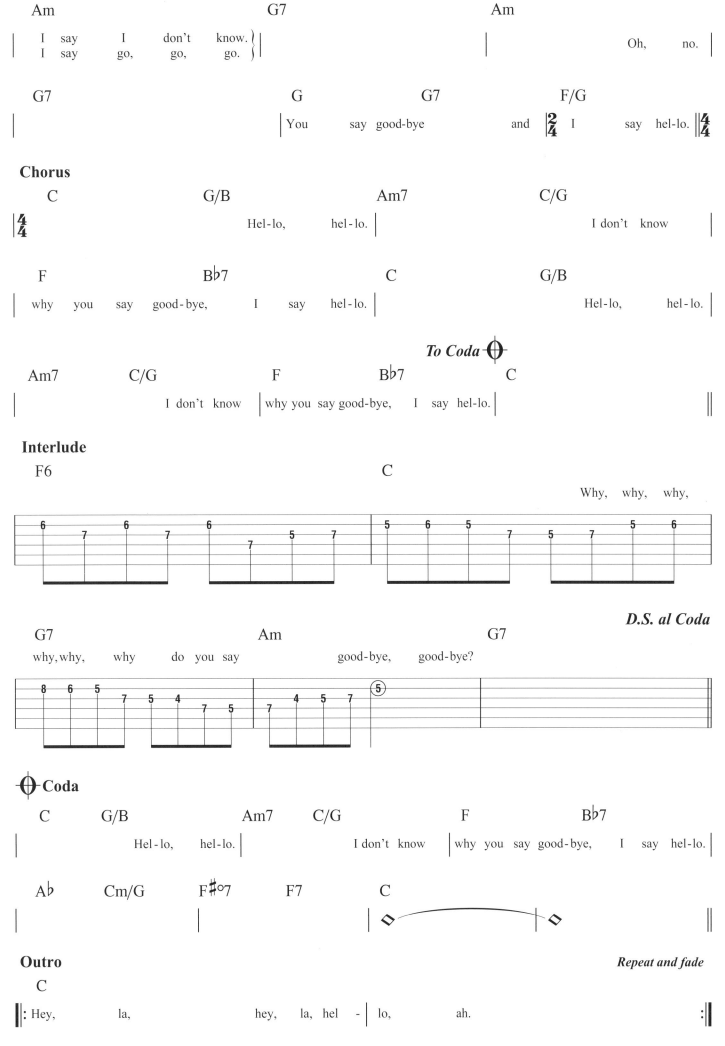

Help!

Words and Music by John Lennon and Paul McCartney

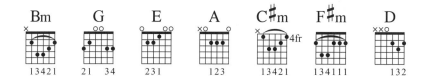

Key of A
Intro
Fast

Strum

Bm
|4/4 Help!   I | need some-bod - y! | Help!   Not just |

G

E
| an - y - bod - y. | Help!   You know I | need   some - one. |

A   **N.C.**

Help!

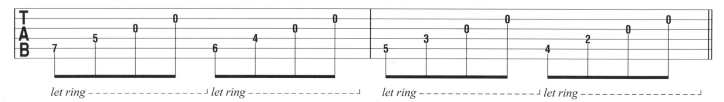

let ring ---------------- *let ring* ---------------- *let ring* ---------------- *let ring* ----------------

Verse

A   **C#m**
‖: 1. When I   was | young - er so   much | young - er than   to - |
   2. And now my | life has changed in | oh, so man - y ways. |

F#m
| day, | I nev - er need - ed | an - y - bod - y's |
| My in - de - | pen - dence seems to |

D   **G**   **A**
| help in an - y way. | | But now these |
| van - ish in the haze. | | But ev - 'ry |

C#m
| days are gone and I'm | not so self - as - | sured. |
| now and then   I | feel so in - se - | cure. |

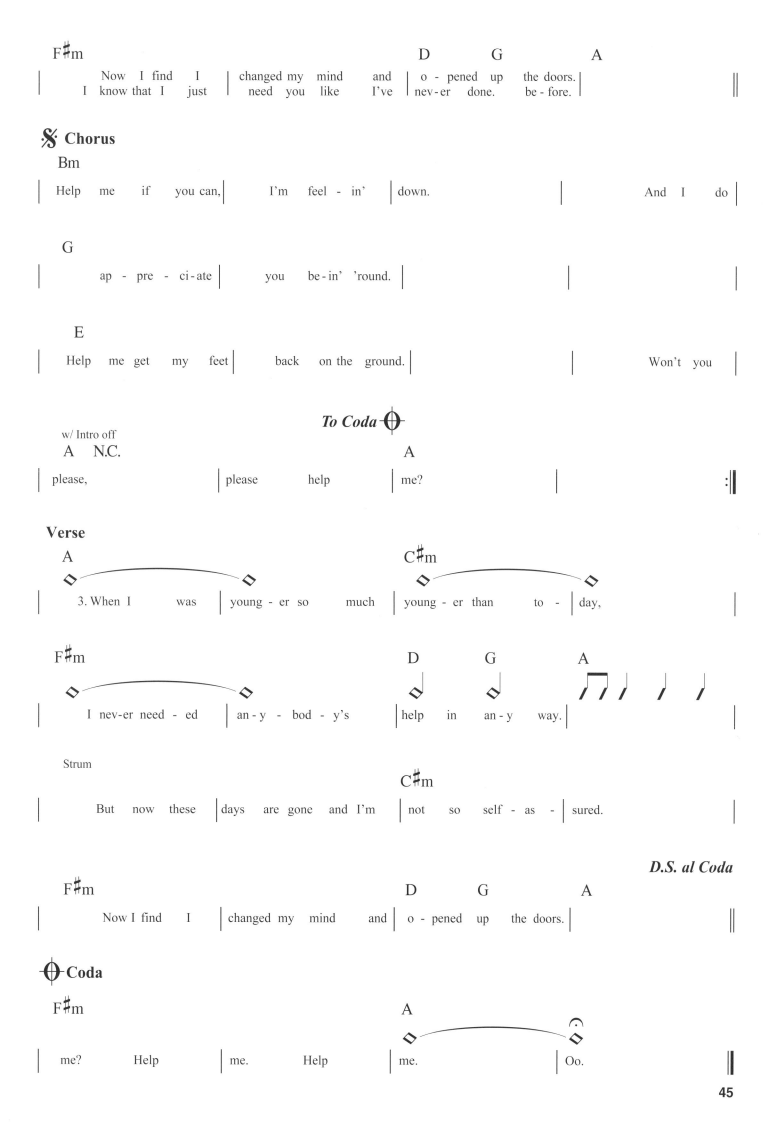

F#m   **D**   **G**   **A**

Now I find I | changed my mind and | o - pened up the doors.

I know that I just | need you like I've | nev-er done. be - fore.

𝄋 Chorus

Bm

Help me if you can, | I'm feel - in' | down. | And I do |

G

ap - pre - ci - ate | you be-in' 'round. | | |

E

Help me get my feet | back on the ground. | | Won't you |

To Coda ⊕

w/ Intro off
A   N.C.   **A**

please, | please help | me? | 𝄇

Verse

A   **C#m**

3. When I was | young - er so much | young - er than to - | day,

F#m   **D**   **G**   **A**

I nev-er need - ed | an - y - bod - y's | help in an - y way. |

Strum   **C#m**

But now these | days are gone and I'm | not so self - as - | sured. |

D.S. al Coda

F#m   **D**   **G**   **A**

Now I find I | changed my mind and | o - pened up the doors. |

⊕ Coda

F#m   **A**

me? Help | me. Help | me. | Oo.

Helter Skelter

Words and Music by John Lennon and Paul McCartney

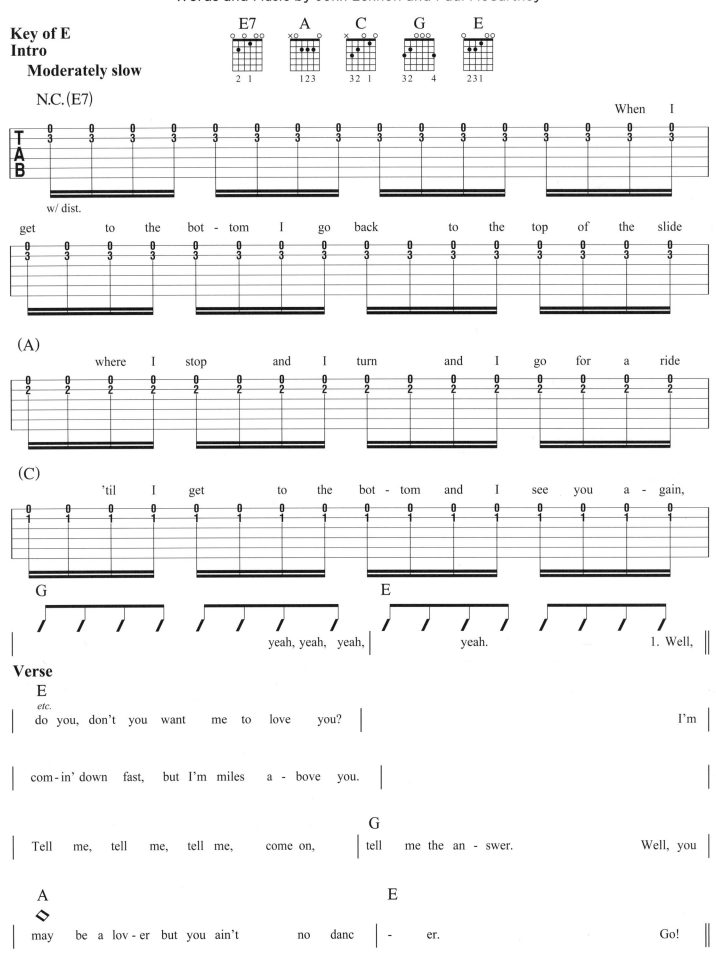

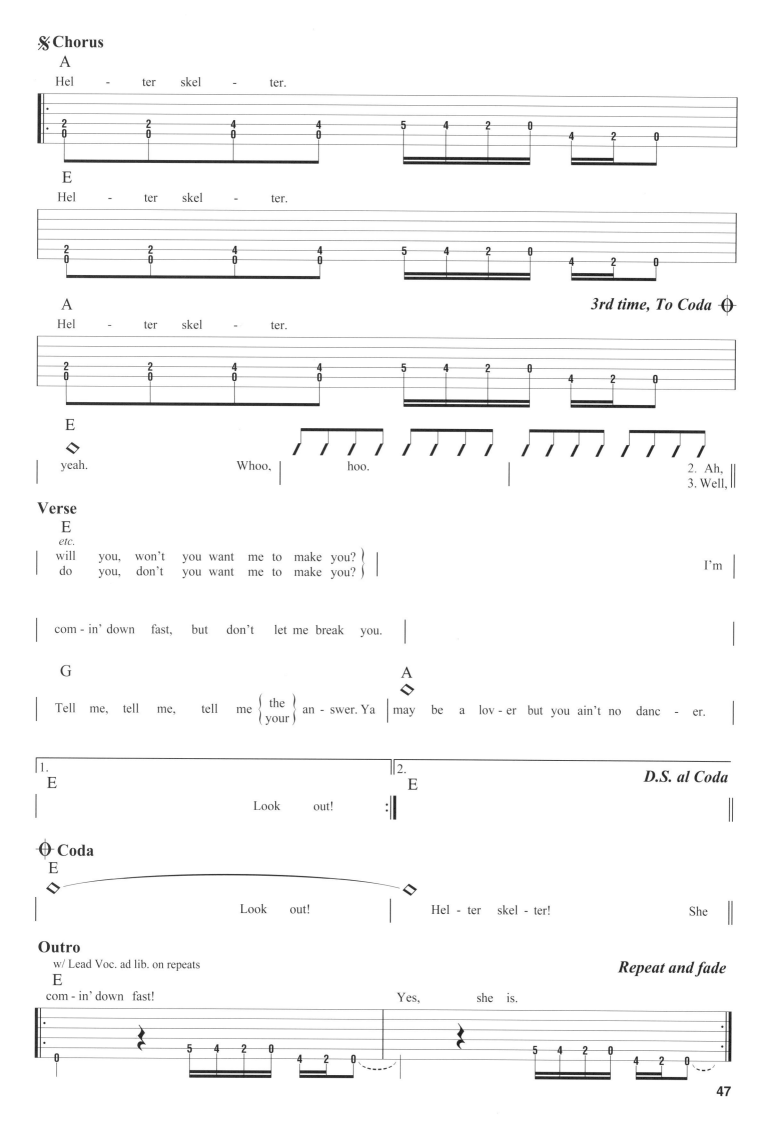

Here, There and Everywhere

Words and Music by John Lennon and Paul McCartney

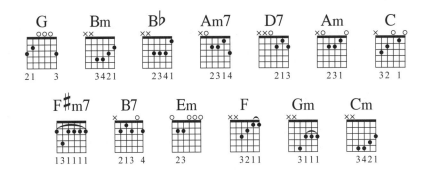

Key of G
Intro
Freely

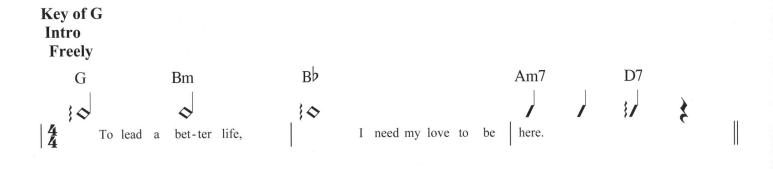

To lead a bet-ter life, I need my love to be here.

Verse
Moderately slow

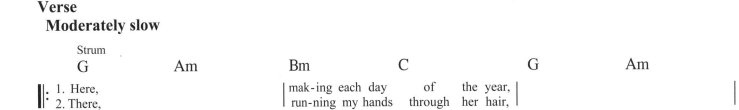

Strum

| G | Am | Bm | C | G | Am |

1. Here, mak-ing each day of the year,
2. There, run-ning my hands through her hair,

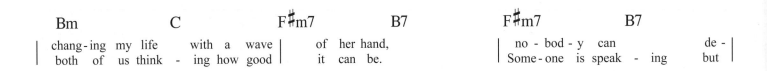

| Bm | C | F#m7 | B7 | F#m7 | B7 |

chang-ing my life with a wave of her hand, no-bod-y can de-
both of us think - ing how good it can be. Some-one is speak-ing but

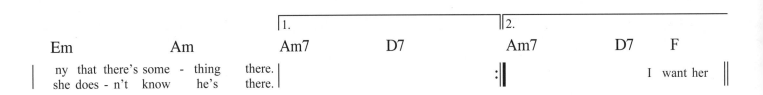

| Em | Am | 1. Am7 | D7 | 2. Am7 | D7 | F |

ny that there's some - thing there.
she does - n't know he's there. I want her

Bridge

Bb	Gm	Cm	D7	Gm

‖: ev - 'ry-where, and if | she's be - side me, I know I need | nev - er care. |

Verse

Cm	D7	G	Am	Bm	C

| But to love her is to need her ‖ 3., 4. ev - 'ry - where, | know - ing that love is to share, |

G	Am	Bm	C	F#m7	B7

| each one be - liev - ing that love | nev - er dies, |

F#m7	B7	Em	Am	Am7	D7	F

1.

| watch-ing her eyes and | hop-ing I'm al - ways there. | I want her :‖

2.

Outro

Am7	D7	G	Am	Bm	C

| I will be ‖ there and | ev - 'ry-where, |

G	Am	Bm	C	G

| here, there and | ev - 'ry-where. |

Hey Jude

Words and Music by John Lennon and Paul McCartney

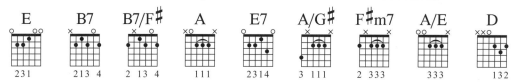

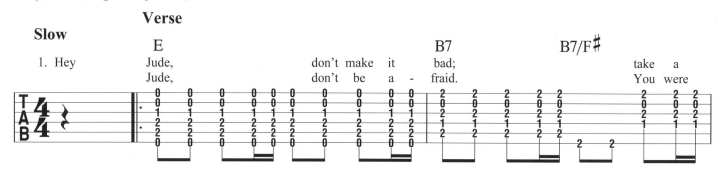

Capo I

Key of F (Capo Key of E)

Verse

Slow

E — B7 — B7/F#

1. Hey Jude, don't make it bad; take a
Jude, don't be a - fraid. You were

B7 — B7/F# — E — A

etc.
sad song and make it | bet - ter. Re - | mem-ber to let her in - to your
made to go out and | get her. The | min - ute you let her un - der your

E — B7 — B7/F#

| heart; then you can start | to make it bet -
| skin, then you be - gin | to make it bet -

1.
E
| ter. 2. Hey :|

2.
E — E7
| ter. And an - y-time you feel the pain,

Bridge

A — A/G# — F#m7 — A/E

‖: hey Jude, re - frain; don't car - ry the world
hey Jude, be - gin; you're wait - ing for some -

B7 — E

| - up - on your shoul | - ders.
| - one to per - form | with.

E7 — A — A/G#

| For well you know that it's a fool | who plays it cool
| And don't you know that it's just you? | Hey Jude, you'll do.

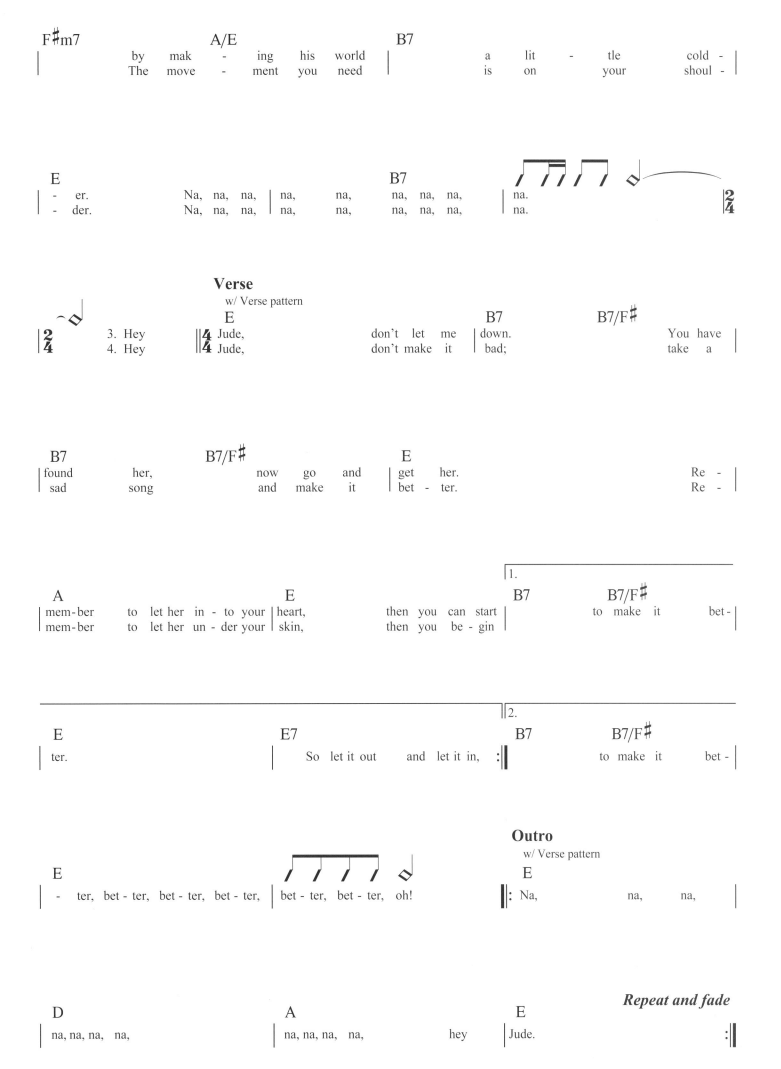

I Feel Fine

Words and Music by John Lennon and Paul McCartney

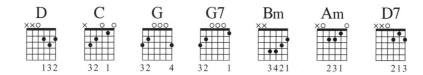

Key of G
Intro
Moderately

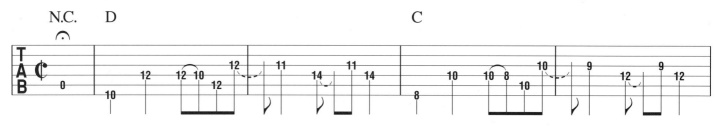

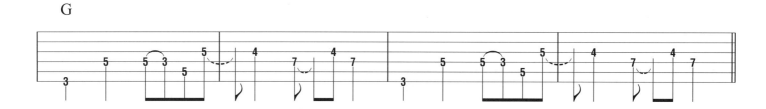

 Verse

Strum
G7

| 1. Ba - by's good to me, | you know, she's hap | - py as can be, |
| 2., 3. Ba - by says she's mine, | you know she tells | me all the time, |

D

| you know she said | so. | |
| you know she said | so. | |

C   **G**

| I'm in love with her | and I feel | fine. |

Chorus

G   **Bm**   **C**   **D**

| I'm so | glad that | she's my lit-tle girl. |

| G   Bm   Am   D7
| She's   so | glad,   she's | tell - ing   all   the world. | 3. That   her   ba - ||

Verse

G7

| -   by   buys   her things, | you know,   he | buys   her   dia - mond rings, | you know,   she said |

To Coda ⊕

D   C

| so. | | She's   in   love   with me | and   I   feel |

Guitar Solo

G   G7

| fine. | ‖ | |

w/ Intro riff

                                                        D

| | | | | | | |

D.S. al Coda
(no repeat)

C   G

| | | | | | ‖

⊕ **Coda**

G   D   C

| fine. | | She's   in   love   with me | and   I   feel |

Outro   *Repeat and fade*

G   G

| fine. | Mm. ‖: | | Mm. :‖

53

I Saw Her Standing There

Words and Music by John Lennon and Paul McCartney

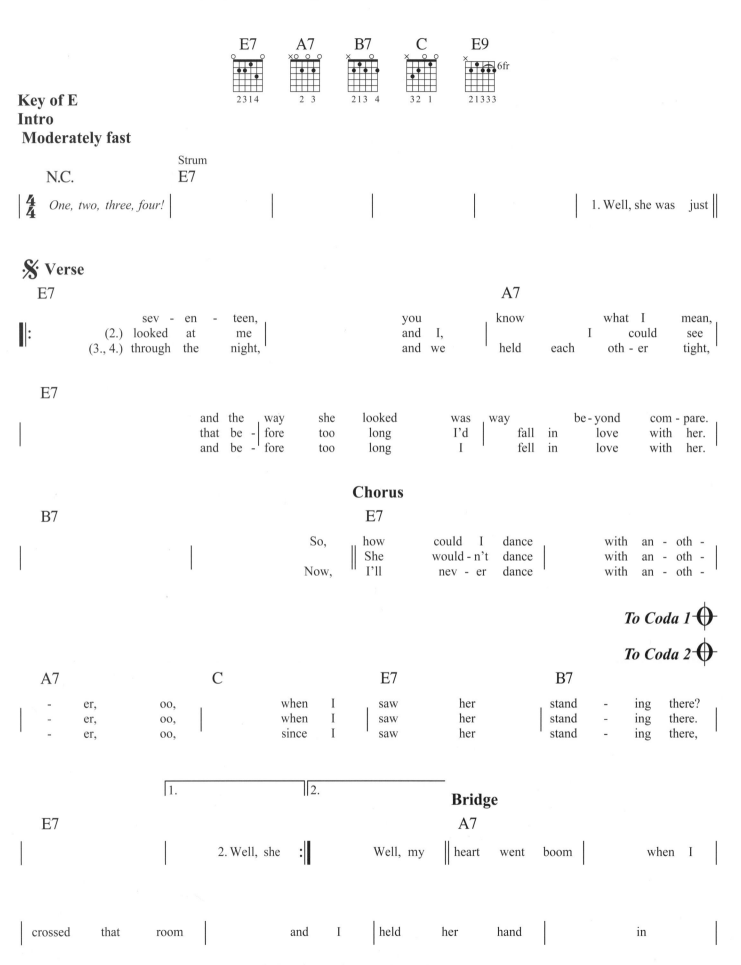

D.S. al Coda 1

B7				A7			
mine.						3. Oh, we danced	

⊕ Coda 1

Guitar Solo

E7		E7					
wow!							

		B7		E7			

A7		E7	B7	E7			
						Well, my	

Bridge

A7							
heart went boom		when I	crossed that room		and I	

		B7					
held her hand		in	mine.			

D.S. al Coda 2   ⊕ **Coda 2**

A7		E7				
4. Oh, we danced				whoa, since I	

Outro

E7	B7				
saw her	stand - ing there.			Yeah, well, since I	

	B7	A7	E7	E9	
saw her	stand - ing there.				

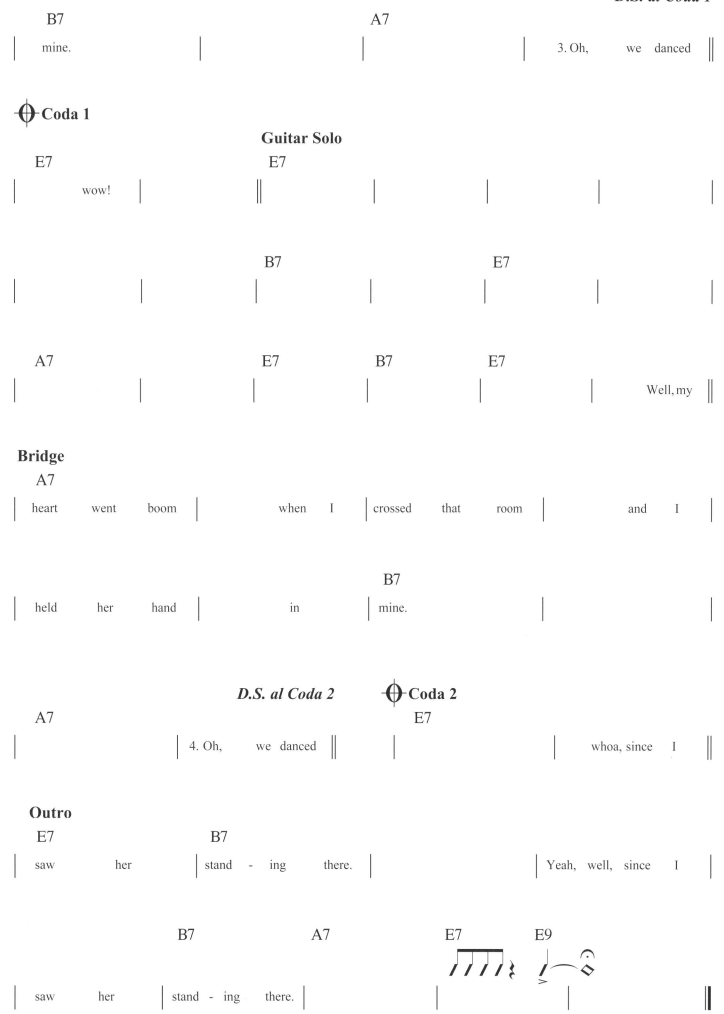

I Want to Hold Your Hand

Words and Music by John Lennon and Paul McCartney

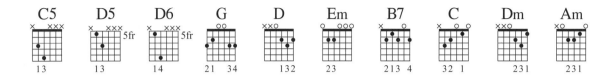

Key of G
Intro
Moderately

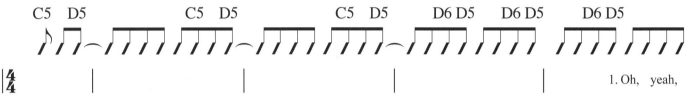

G		**D**		**Em**
I'll	tell you some - thing		I think you'll un - der -
please	say to me		you'll let me be your
you	got that some - thing		I think you'll un - der -

B7		**G**		**D**
stand.	When	I	say that some - thing,	
man.	And	please	say to me	
stand.	When	I	say that some - thing,	

Chorus

Em		**B7**	**C**	**D**	**G**	**Em**
I wan-na hold your hand.			I wan-na	hold your	hand.
you'll let me hold your hand.			Now let me	hold your	hand.
I wan-na hold your hand.			I wan-na		

C	**D**	**1. G**	**2. G**
I wan-na hold your		hand. 2. Oh,	hand.

Bridge

Dm			G			C		Am	
	And	when	I	touch	you	I	feel	hap-py	in-side.

Dm				G				C		C5	D5
	It's	just	a	feel	-	ing	that	my	love,	I	can't hide,

To Coda ⊕   ***D.S. al Coda***
(take 2nd ending)

C5	D5		C5	D5	D6 D5	D6 D5	D6 D5	
	I can't hide,		I can't hide.				3. Yeah,	

⊕ Coda

Verse

D6	D5		G		D	
	4. Yeah,	you	got that	some - thing		

Em		B7		G	
	I think you'll un - der -	stand.	When	I	feel that

D		Em		B7	
	some - thing,		I wan - na hold	your hand.	

Outro-Chorus

C	D	G	Em	C	D	B7	
	I wan - na hold your	hand.			I wan - na hold your	hand.	

C	D	C		G	
	I wan - na hold your	hand.			

I Will

Words and Music by John Lennon and Paul McCartney

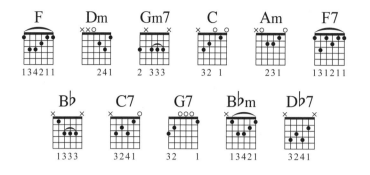

Key of F

Verse

Moderately

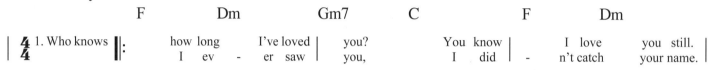

F	Dm	Gm7	C	F	Dm

4/4 1. Who knows ‖: how long I've loved you? You know I love you still.
I ev - er saw you, I did - n't catch your name.

Am	F7	B♭	C7	Dm	F

Will I wait a lone - ly life - time? If you want
But it nev - er real - ly mat - tered; I will al -

1. | B♭ C7 | F Dm | Gm7 C7 | **2.** F F7 |

B♭ C7 | F Dm | Gm7 C7 | F F7

me to, I will.
- ways feel the same. 2. For if :‖

Bridge

B♭	Am	Dm	Gm7	C7	F	F7

Love you for - ev - er and for-ev - er, love you with all my heart.

B♭	Am	Dm	G7	C7

Love you when-ev - er we're to-geth - er, love you when we're a - part. 3. And when

Verse

F	Dm	Gm7	C7	F	Dm
at last	I find	you,	your song	will fill	the air.

Am	F7	B♭	C7	Dm B♭m	F
Sing it loud	so I	can hear	you,	make it eas -	

B♭	C7	Dm B♭m	F	B♭	C7
- y to	be near	you	for the things	you do	en - dear

Dm B♭m F	Gm7	C7	D♭7	
you to me. Ah,	you know	I will.		

F		F7 B♭ Am	
I will.		Mm, mm.	

Dm	Gm7 C7	F	
	Da, da, da, da, la, la.		

59

In My Life

Words and Music by John Lennon and Paul McCartney

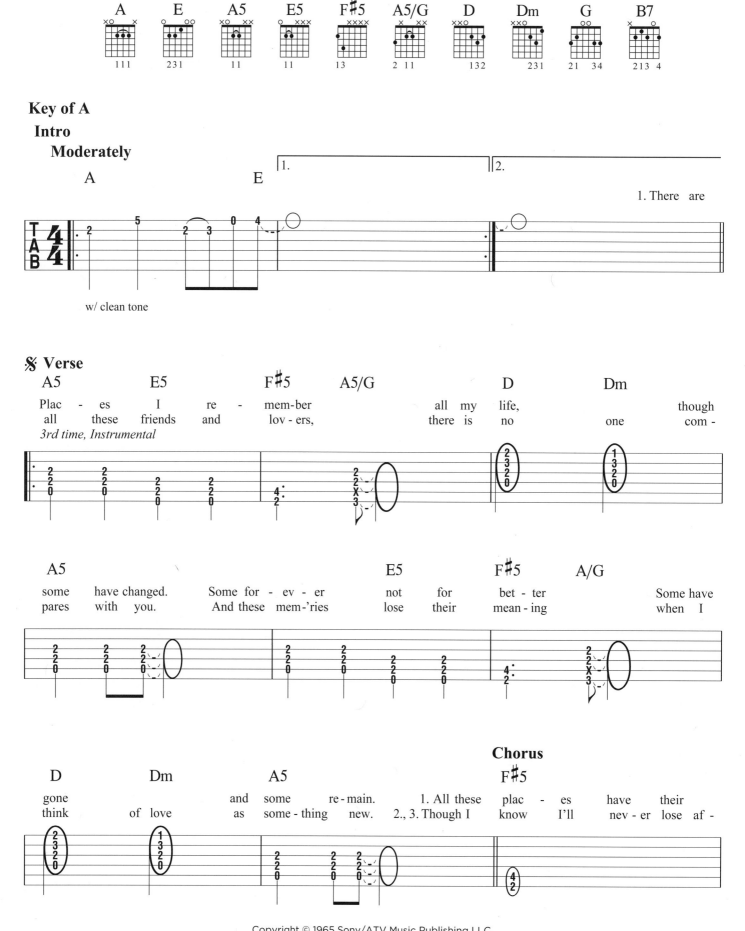

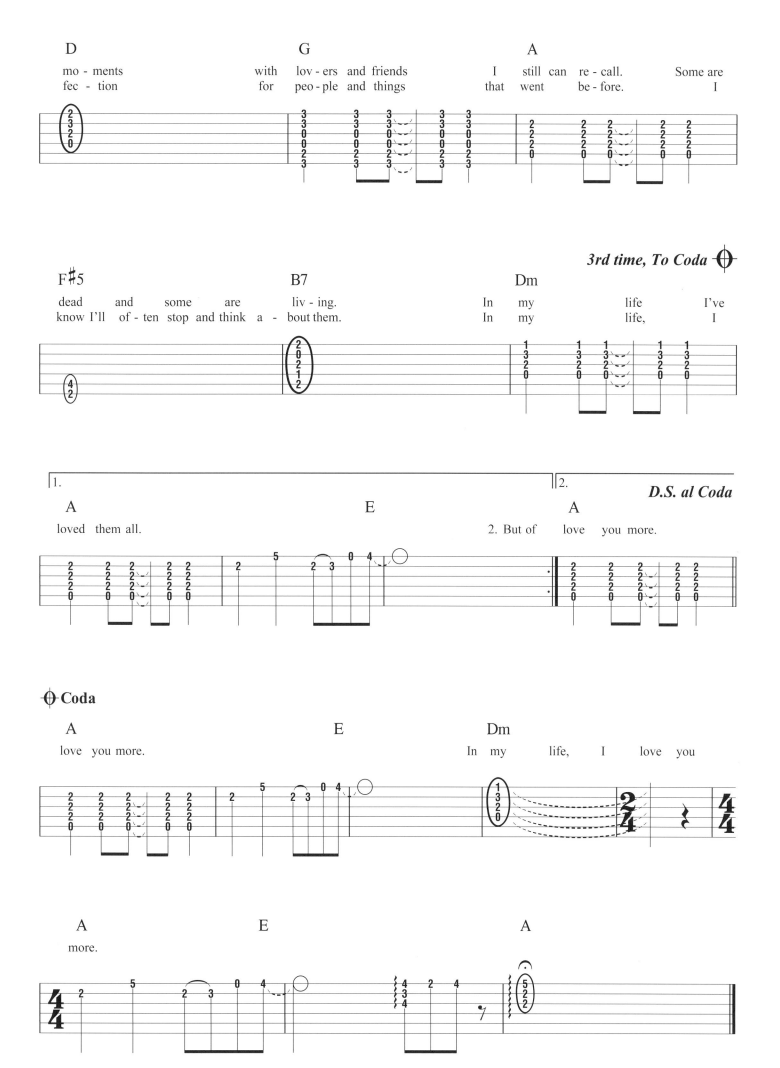

Lady Madonna

Words and Music by John Lennon and Paul McCartney

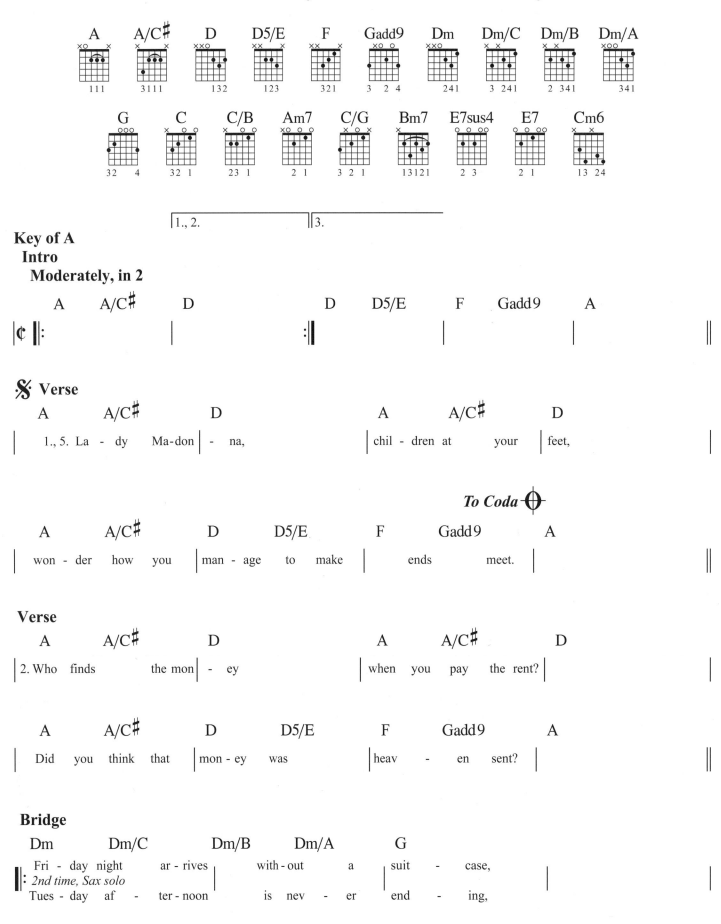

C	C/B	Am7	C/G	Am7

Sun - day morn - ing,	creep - ing like a	nun.		
Wednes - day morn - ing,	pa - pers did - n't	come.		

Dm	Dm/C	Dm/B	Dm/A	G

Mon - day's child has	learned to tie his	boot - lace.	*Solo ends*
Thurs - day night your	stock - ing need - ed	mend - ing.	

3rd time, D.S. al Coda ⌖

C	Bm7	E7sus4	E7

See	how they	run.		

Verse

A	A/C♯	D	A	A/C♯	D

3. La - dy Ma - don	- na,	ba - by at your	breast
4. La - dy Ma - don	- na,	ly - ing on the bed,	

A	A/C♯	D	D5/E	F	Gadd9	A

won - ders how you	man - age to feed	the rest.
lis - ten to the mu	- sic play - ing	in your head.

Interlude

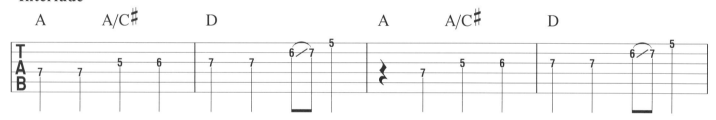

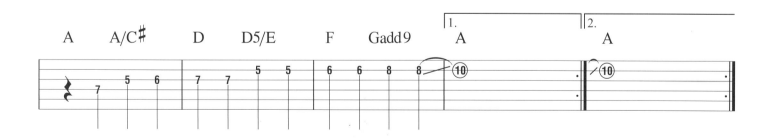

⌖**Coda**

Let It Be

Words and Music by John Lennon and Paul McCartney

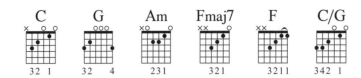

 Key of C
Intro
Slow

|C|G|Am|Fmaj7|C|G|F|C|
|||||||| 1. When I

𝄋 Verse

C		G		Am		Fmaj7	
find	my-self	in	times	of	trou-ble,	Moth-er Mar - y	comes to me
3. *Guitar solo*							

| C | | G | | F | | C | |
| speak-ing | words | of | wis-dom, | let it be. | | | And |

| | G | | Am | | Fmaj7 | |
| in my | hour | of dark-ness, | she is stand-|ing | right in | front of me, |

| C | | G | | F | | C | |
| speak-ing | words | of | wis-dom, | let it be. | | *Solo ends* } | Let it be, |

Chorus

| Am | | C/G | | F | | C | |
| | let it be, | | let it be, | | let it be. | | |

	G		F		C	
	Whis-per words	of wis-dom,	let it be.		2. And
						4. And

Verse

C		G		Am		Fmaj7	
when	the brok-en	heart-ed	peo-ple	liv-ing in	the world	a-gree,
when	the night	is cloud-y,	there is	still a light	that shines	on me.

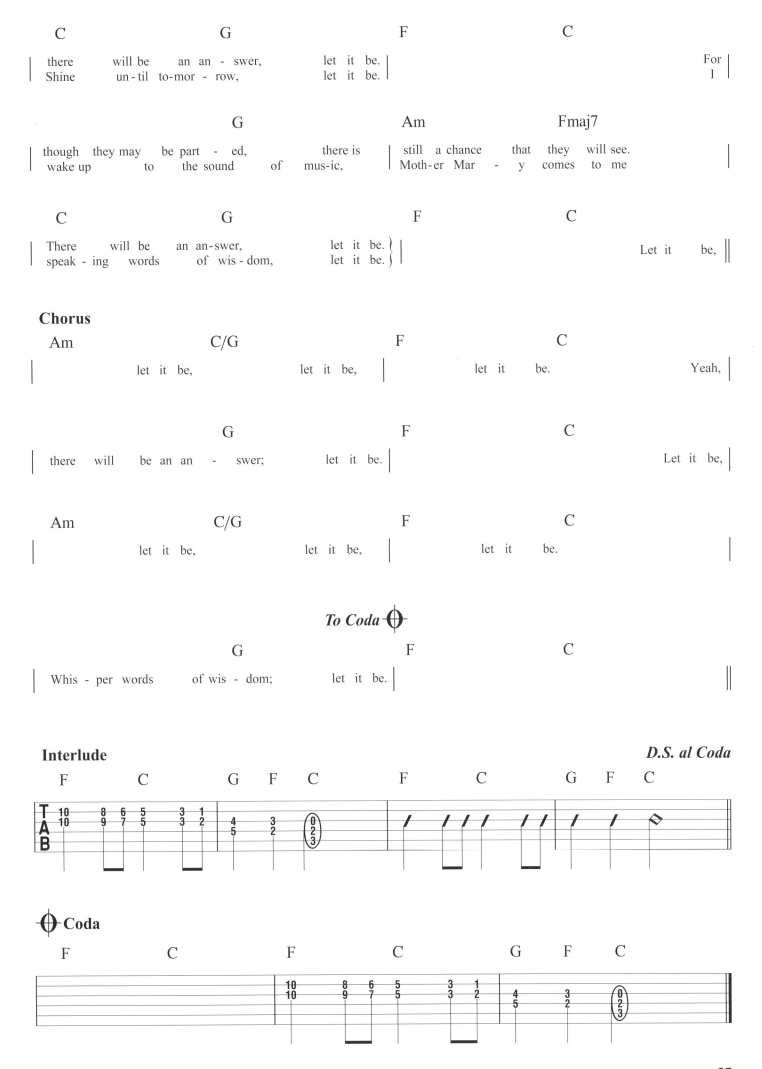

C	G		F	C

there   will be   an an - swer,   let it be.   For
Shine   un - til to-mor - row,   let it be.   I

	G	Am	Fmaj7

though they may   be part - ed,   there is   still a chance   that   they   will see.
wake up   to   the sound   of   mus-ic,   Moth-er Mar   -   y   comes   to   me

C	G		F	C

There   will be   an an-swer,   let it be.   Let it   be,
speak - ing   words   of wis - dom,   let it be.

Chorus

Am	C/G	F	C

         let it be,   let it be,   let it   be.   Yeah,

	G	F	C

there   will   be an an - swer;   let it be.   Let it be,

Am	C/G	F	C

         let it be,   let it be,   let it   be.

To Coda ⊕

	G	F	C

Whis - per words   of wis - dom;   let it be.

Interlude   *D.S. al Coda*

⊕ **Coda**

Love Me Do

Words and Music by John Lennon and Paul McCartney

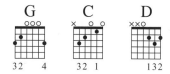

Key of G
Intro
Moderately

G		C		G		C	

| **4/4** | | | | | | | |

G		C		G			

𝄋 Chorus

G		C		G		C	
Love,	love me do.		You	know	I love you.		I'll

G		C					
al - ways be true.		So,	please				

To Coda 1 ⊕

To Coda 2 ⊕

N.C.		G		C		G	
	love me	do.		Whoa,	love	me do.	

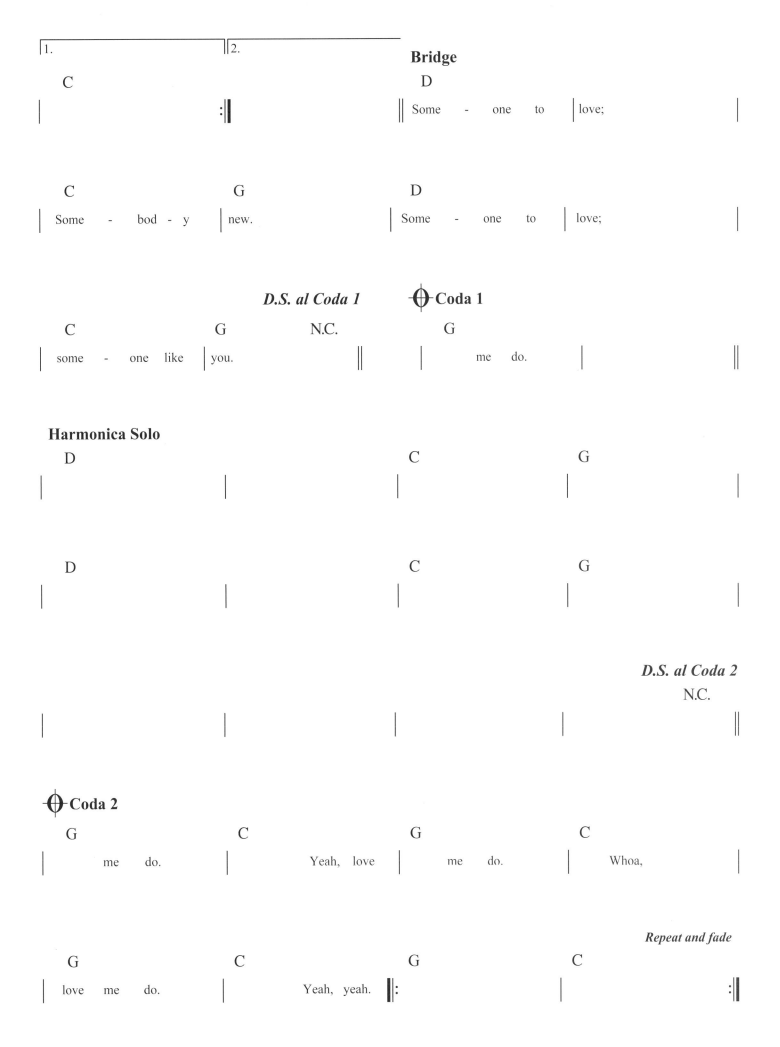

Lucy in the Sky with Diamonds

Words and Music by John Lennon and Paul McCartney

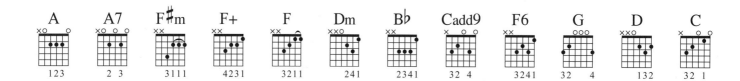

Key of A
Intro
Moderately

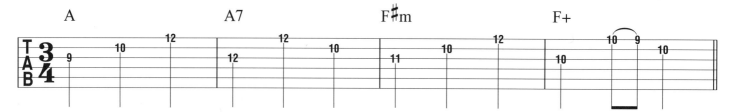

𝄋 **Verse**

1. Pic - ture your - self in a boat on a riv - er, with tan - ger - ine
2. Fol - low her down to a bridge by a foun - tain where rock - ing horse
3. Pic - ture your - self on a train in a sta - tion, with plas - ti - cine

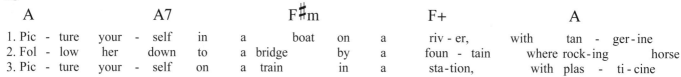

trees and mar - ma - lade skies. Some - bod - y calls
peo - ple eat marsh - mal - low pies. Ev - 'ry - one
port - ers with look - ing glass ties. Sud - den - ly

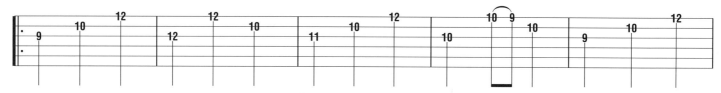

To Coda ⊕

you, you an - swer quite slow - ly. A girl with ka - lei - do - scope
smiles as you drift past the flow - ers, that grow so in - cred - i - bly
some - one is there at the turn - stile, the girl with ka - lei - do - scope

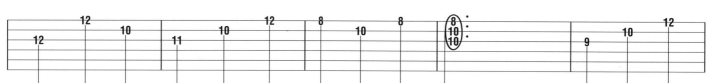

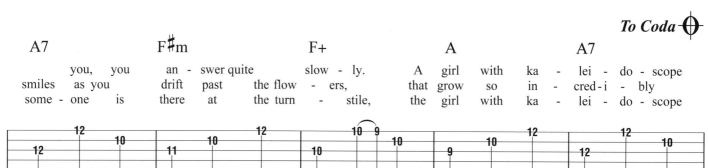

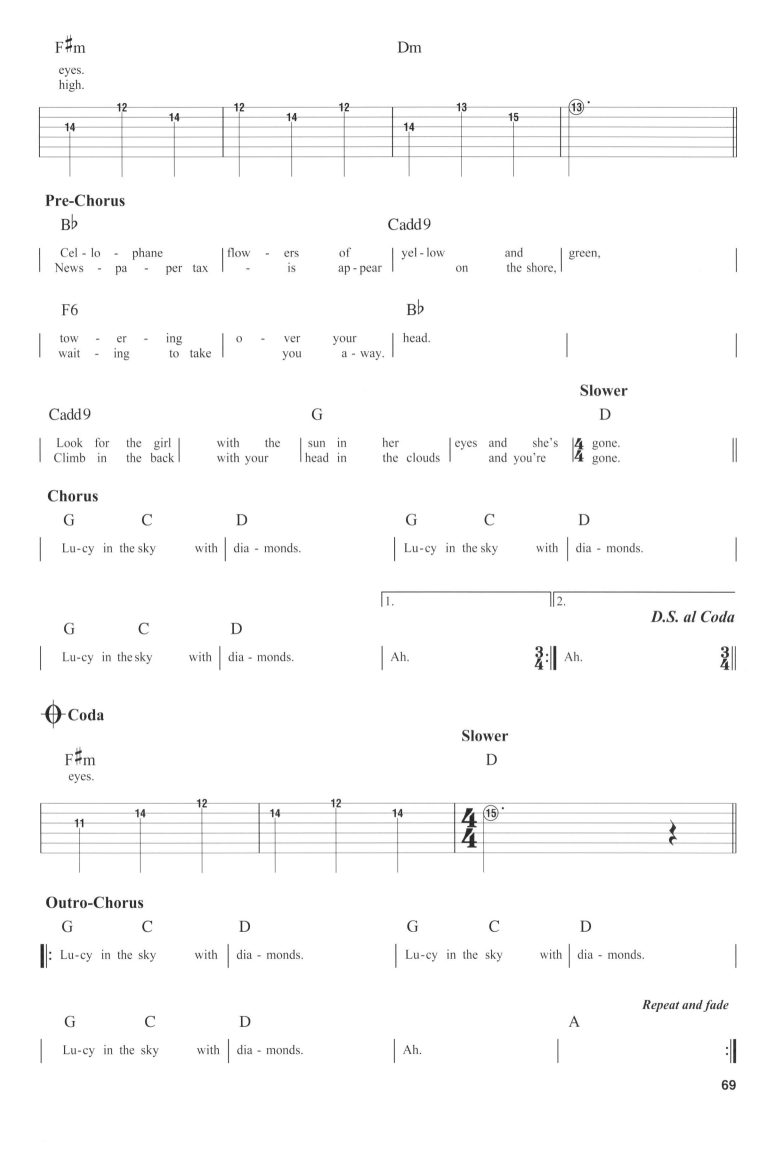

Michelle

Words and Music by John Lennon and Paul McCartney

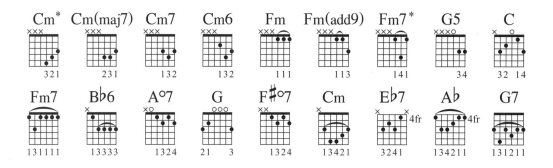

Capo V

Key of F (Capo Key of C)
Intro
Moderately

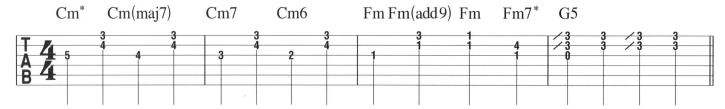

Chorus

Strum

| C | | Fm7 | | Bb6 |
| Mi - chelle | | ma belle, | | these are words that |

| A°7 | | G | F#°7 | G |
| go to - geth - er | | well, | my Mi-chelle. | |

| C | | Fm7 | | Bb6 |
| Mi - chelle, | | ma belle, | | sont les mots qui |

| A°7 | | G | F#°7 | G | |
| vont tres bien en - | semble, | | tres bien en - | semble. | 1. I
2. I |

⅀ Verse

Cm					Eb7
love you, I love you, I	love you,			that's all I want to
need to, I need to, I	need to,			I need to make you
want you, I want you, I	want you,			I think you know by

Ab		G7		Cm
say.		Un - til I find a way,		I will
see,		oh, what you mean to	me.	Un -
now.		I'll get to you some - how.		Un -

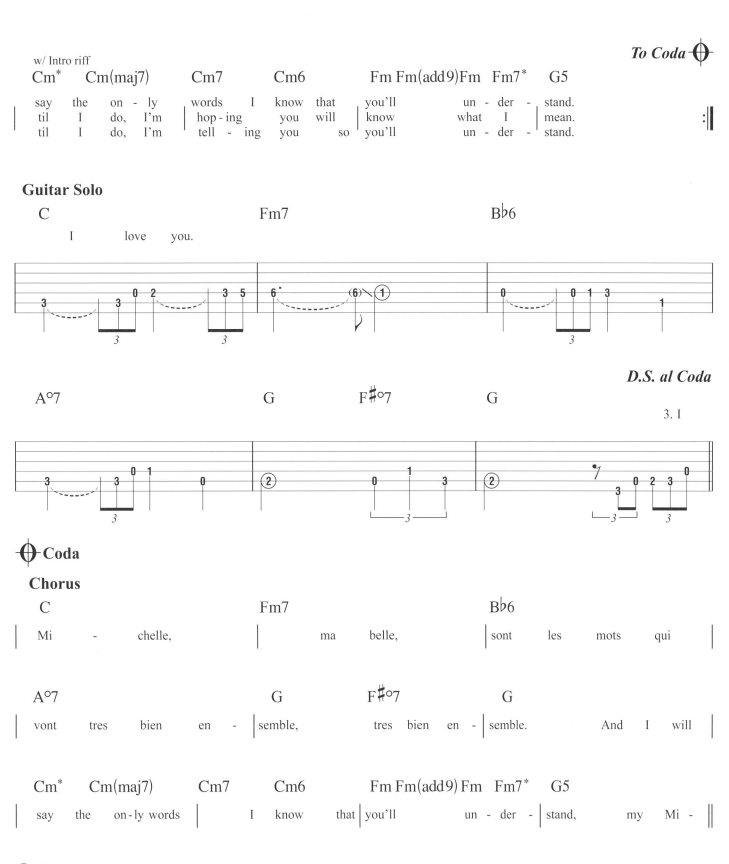

w/ Intro riff

| Cm* | Cm(maj7) | Cm7 | Cm6 | Fm Fm(add9)Fm | Fm7* | G5 |

say the on - ly | words I know that | you'll un - der - stand.
til I do, I'm | hop - ing you will | know what I | mean.
til I do, I'm | tell - ing you so | you'll un - der - stand.

Guitar Solo

C   Fm7   B♭6

I love you.

D.S. al Coda

A°7   G   F♯°7   G

3. I

⊕ **Coda**

Chorus

C   Fm7   B♭6

Mi - chelle, | ma belle, | sont les mots qui |

A°7   G   F♯°7   G

vont tres bien en - | semble, tres bien en - | semble. And I will |

| Cm* | Cm(maj7) | Cm7 | Cm6 | Fm Fm(add9) Fm | Fm7* | G5 |

say the on - ly words | I know that | you'll un - der - | stand, my Mi - |

Outro

w/ Guitar Solo

C   Fm7   B♭6

‖: chelle. | | |
(Sung 1st time only.)

Repeat and fade

A°7   G   F♯°7   G

:‖

Norwegian Wood
(This Bird Has Flown)

Words and Music by John Lennon and Paul McCartney

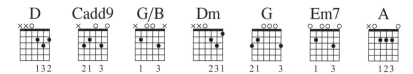

Capo II
Key of E (Capo Key of D)
Intro
Moderately fast

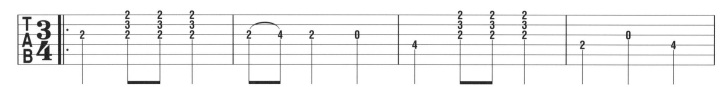

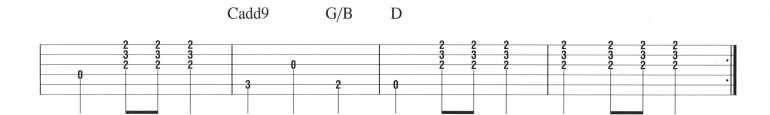

Verse

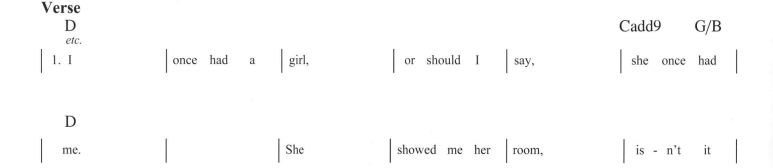

1. I	once had a	girl,	or should I	say,	she once had	

D						
me.		She	showed me her	room,	is - n't it	

§ **Bridge**

good	Nor - we - gian	wood?		She	asked me to	stay and she
					told me she	worked in the

told me to	sit an - y -	where.			So
morn - ing and	start - ed to	laugh.			I

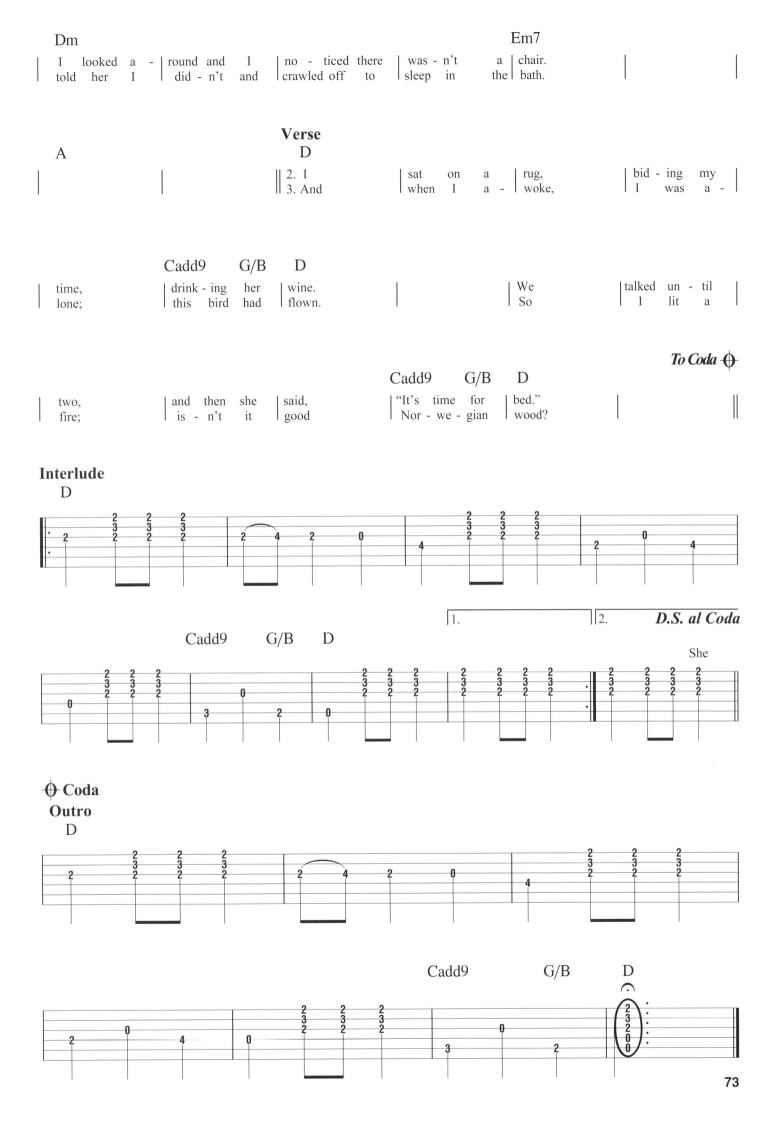

Dm   Em7

I looked a - | round and I | no - ticed there | was - n't   a | chair.
told her I | did - n't and | crawled off to | sleep in   the | bath.

Verse

A   D

2. I | sat   on   a | rug, | bid - ing   my
3. And | when I a - | woke, | I   was a -

Cadd9   G/B   D

time, | drink - ing her | wine. | | We | talked un - til
lone; | this bird had | flown. | | So | I   lit   a

To Coda ⊕

Cadd9   G/B   D

two, | and   then she | said, | "It's time for | bed." | ‖
fire; | is - n't it | good | Nor - we - gian | wood? | ‖

Interlude

D

|1. |2.   *D.S. al Coda*

Cadd9   G/B   D

                                                                She

⊕ **Coda**

Outro

D

Cadd9   G/B   D

73

Nowhere Man

Words and Music by John Lennon and Paul McCartney

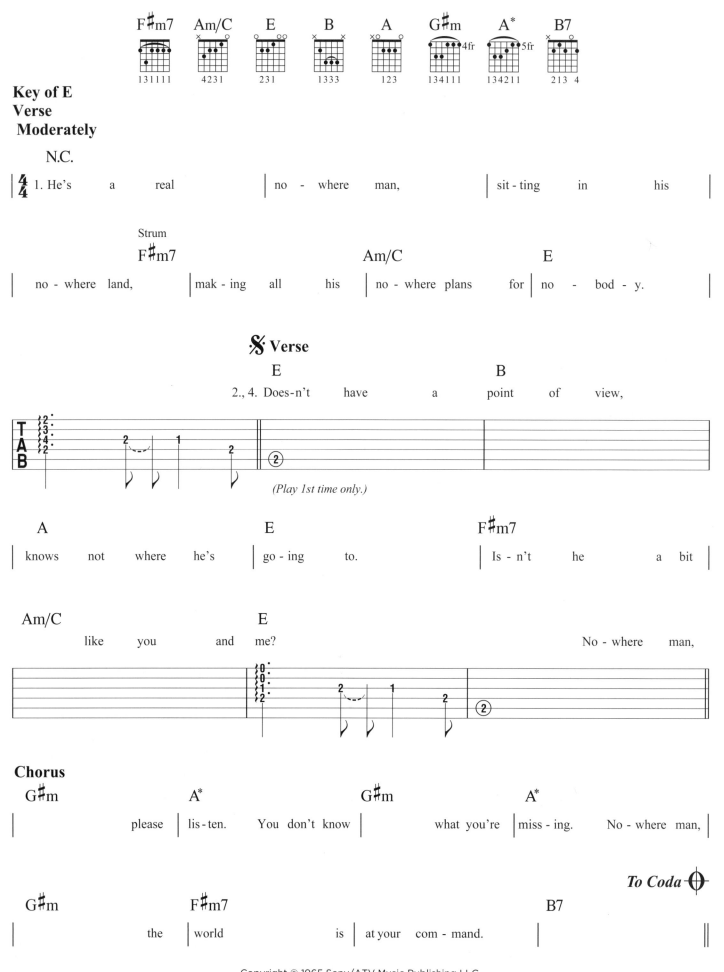

Ob-La-Di, Ob-La-Da

Words and Music by John Lennon and Paul McCartney

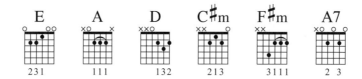

Capo 1

Key of F (Capo key of E)
Intro
Moderately, in 2

Play 8 times

𝄋 Verse

A

1. Des - mond has a | bar - row in the | mar - ket place, | Mol -
2. Des - mond takes a | trol - ley to the | jewel - er's store, | buys

3., 4. *See additional lyrics*

- ly is the | sing - er in a | band. | Des -
  a twen - ty | car - at gold - en | ring. | Takes

- mond says to | Mol - ly, "Girl, I | like your face," | and Mol - ly
  it back to | Mol - ly wait - ing | at the door, | and as he

A   E   A

says this as she | takes him by the hand: | Ob - la - di,
gives it to her | she be - gins to sing:

Chorus

A   C♯m   F♯m

ob - la - da, | life goes on, | bra, | la -

A   E   A

- la, how their | life goes on. | Ob - la - di,

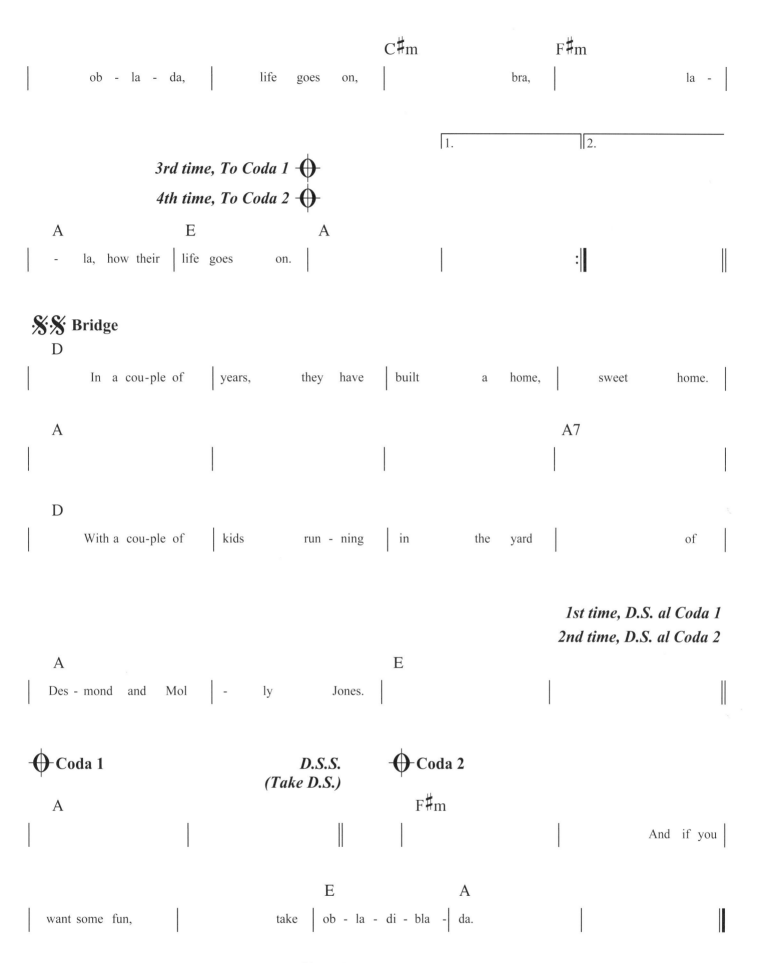

Additional Lyrics

3. Happy ever after in the market place, Desmond lets the children lend a hand.
   Molly stays at home and does her pretty face and in the evening she still sings it with the band.

4. Happy ever after in the market place, Molly lets the children lend a hand.
   Desmond stays at home and does his pretty face and in the evening she's a singer with the band.

Paperback Writer

Words and Music by John Lennon and Paul McCartney

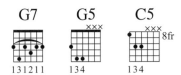

G7   G5   C5

Key of G
Intro
Moderately

N.C.

$\frac{4}{4}$ Pa - per - back   writ - er.
(Pa - per - back   writ - er.)
(Pa - per - back   writ - er.)

N.C.(G7)

1. Dear

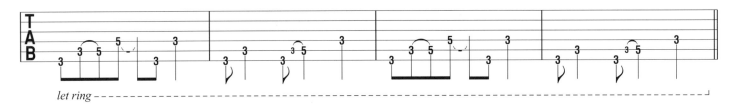

let ring -

𝄋 Verse

Strum
G5

Sir   or   Ma - dam, will you | read   my   book? It took me | years   to write,   will you |
2., 3., 4. *See additional lyrics*

take   a   look?   It's | based   on   a   nov - el   by   a | man   named   Lear.   And I |

C5

need   a   job,   so I | want to be a pa - per - back | writ - er, | pa - per - back |

1., 3.
N.C.(G7)

writ - er.

2., 4.
N.C.(G7)

2. It's a   writ - er.

let ring -   *let ring - - - - - - - - - - - - - - - -*

Interlude

N.C.

Pa - per - back   writ - er.
(Pa - per - back   writ - er.)
(Pa - per - back   writ - er.)

D.S. al Coda
(take repeat)

3. It's a

N.C.(G7)

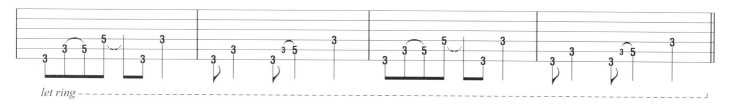

let ring -

 Coda

N.C.(G7)

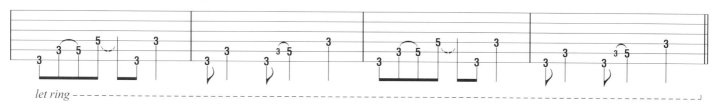

let ring -

Outro

Repeat and fade

G5

(Pa - per - back   writ - er.)   Pa - per - back   writ - er.

Additional Lyrics

2. It's a dirty story of a dirty man,
   And his clinging wife doesn't understand.
   His son is working for the Daily Mail.
   It's a steady job, but he wants to be a paperback writer,
   Paperback writer.

3. It's a thousand pages, give or take a few;
   I'll be writing more in a week or two.
   I can make it longer, if you like the style.
   I can change it 'round, and I want to be a paperback writer,
   Paperback writer.

4. If you really like it, you can have the rights.
   It could make a million for you overnight.
   If you must return it, you can send it here.
   But I need a break, and I want to be a paperback writer,
   Paperback writer.

Penny Lane

Words and Music by John Lennon and Paul McCartney

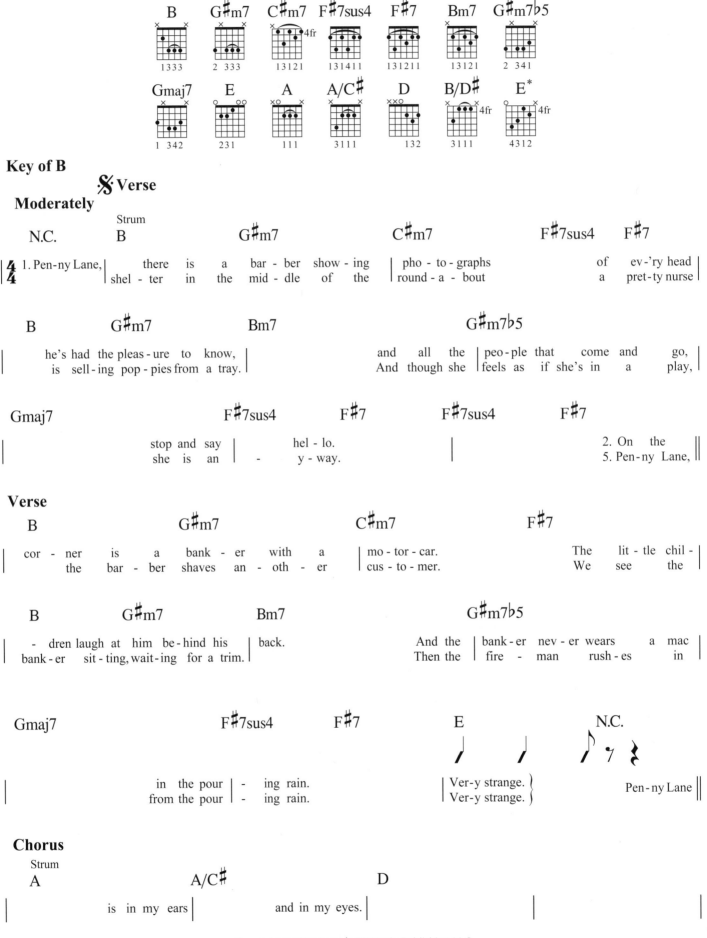

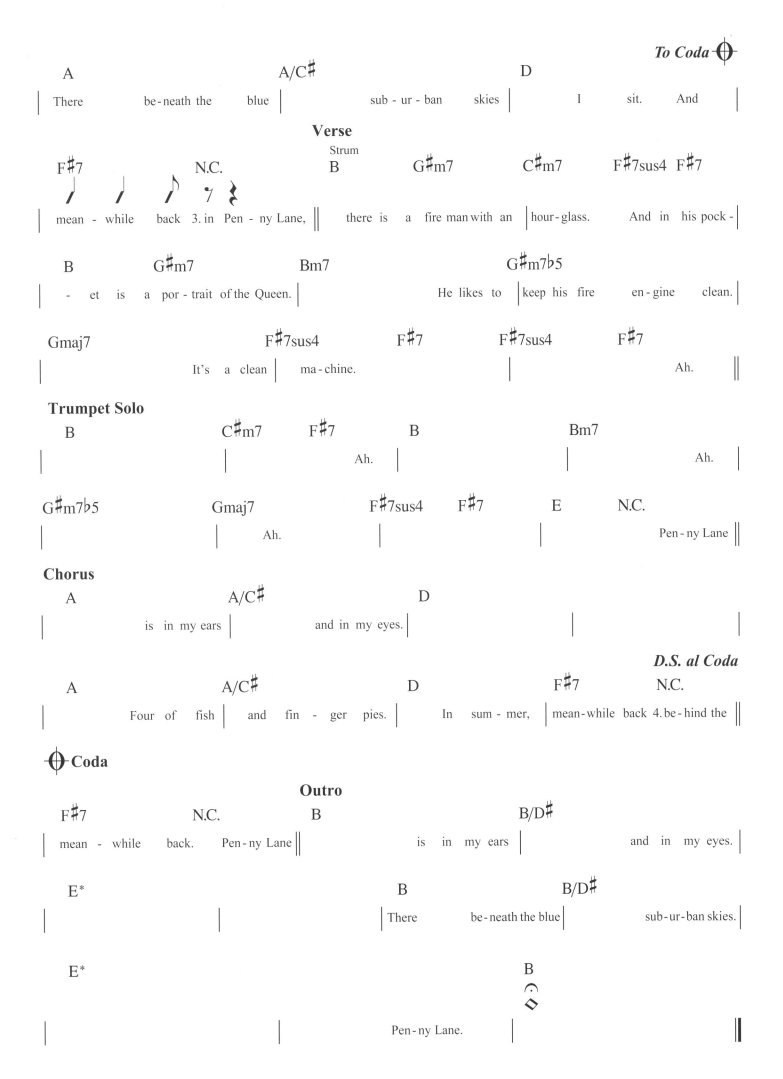

Revolution

Words and Music by John Lennon and Paul McCartney

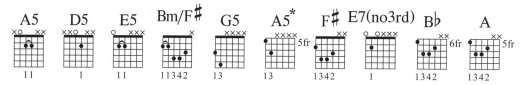

Tune up approx. 1 step (A = 481 Hz):
(low to high) F♯-B-E-A-C♯-F♯

Key of A

Intro

Moderately

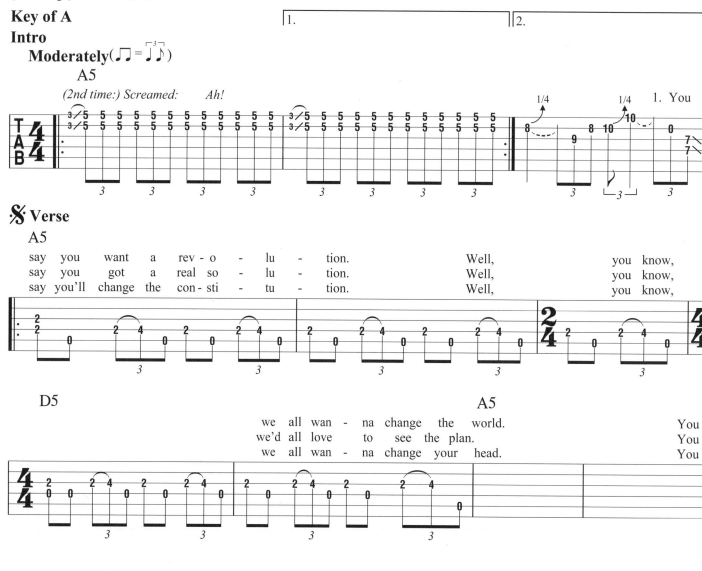

(2nd time:) Screamed: Ah!

Verse

say you want a rev-o-lu-tion.	Well,	you know,
say you got a real so-lu-tion.	Well,	you know,
say you'll change the con-sti-tu-tion.	Well,	you know,

we all wan-na change the world.	You
we'd all love to see the plan.	You
we all wan-na change your head.	You

tell me that it's ev-o-lu-tion.	Well,	you know,
ask me for a con-tri-bu-tion.	Well,	you know,
tell me it's the in-sti-tu-tion.	Well,	you know,

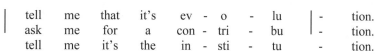

we all wan-na change the world.
we're all do-in' what we can.
you bet-ter free your mind in-stead.

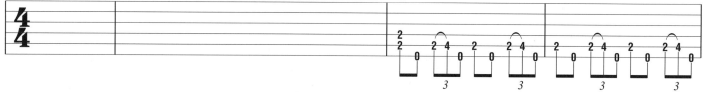

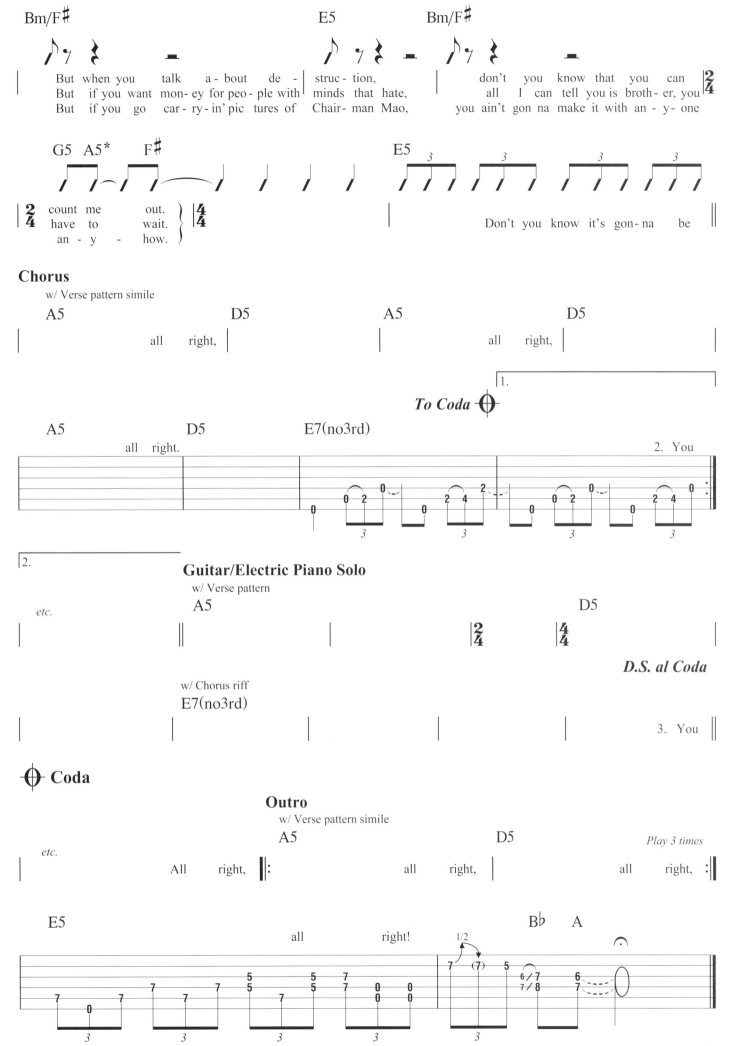

Chorus
w/ Verse pattern simile

Guitar/Electric Piano Solo
w/ Verse pattern

w/ Chorus riff

D.S. al Coda

Coda

Outro
w/ Verse pattern simile

Sgt. Pepper's Lonely Hearts Club Band

Words and Music by John Lennon and Paul McCartney

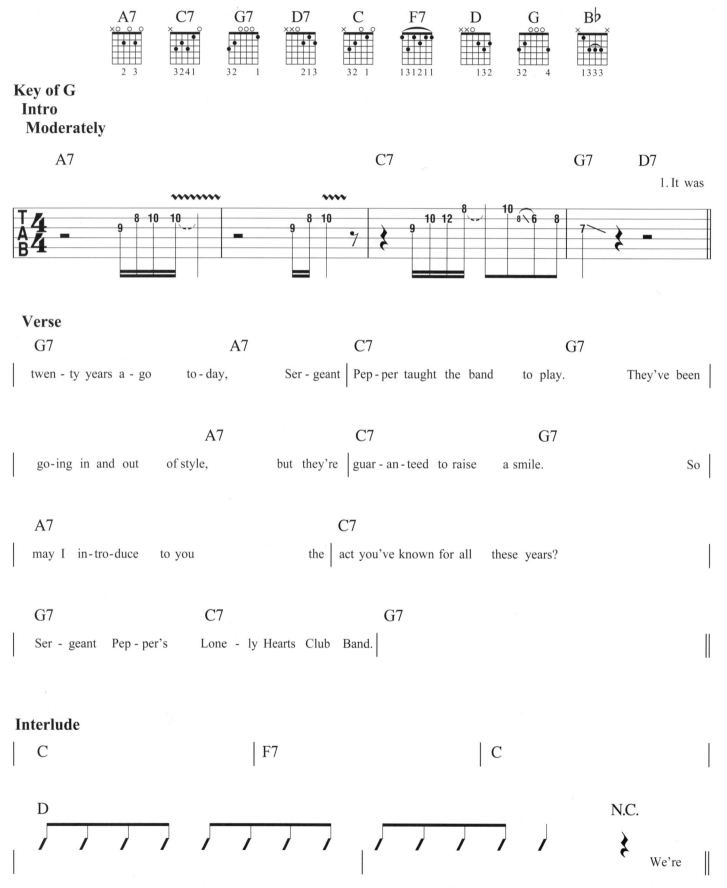

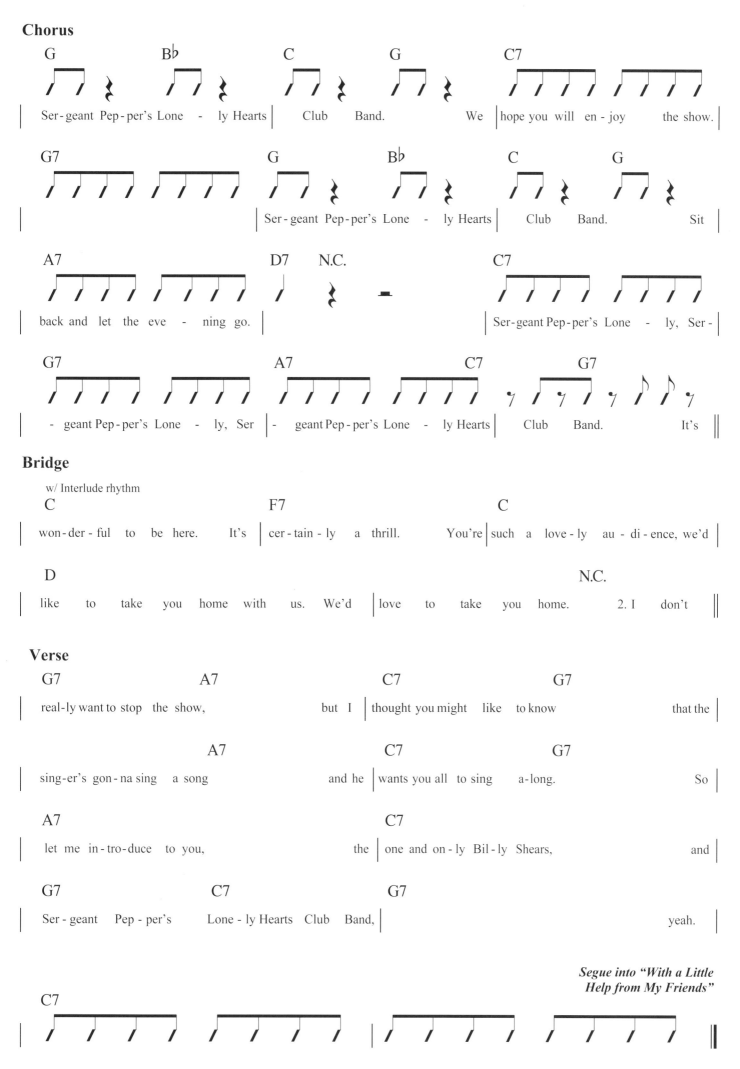

Chorus

G | B♭ | C | G | C7

Ser-geant Pep-per's Lone - ly Hearts | Club   Band.   We | hope you will en-joy   the show. |

G7 | G | B♭ | C | G

| Ser-geant Pep-per's Lone - ly Hearts | Club   Band.   Sit |

A7 | D7   N.C. | C7

back and let the eve - ning go. | | Ser-geant Pep-per's Lone - ly, Ser - |

G7 | A7 | C7   G7

- geant Pep-per's Lone - ly, Ser | - geant Pep-per's Lone - ly Hearts | Club   Band.   It's ‖

Bridge

w/ Interlude rhythm

C | F7 | C

| won-der-ful to be here.   It's | cer-tain-ly a thrill.   You're | such a love-ly au-di-ence, we'd |

D | N.C.

| like   to take you home with us. We'd | love   to take you home.   2. I   don't ‖

Verse

G7   A7 | C7   G7

| real-ly want to stop the show,   but I | thought you might like to know   that the |

A7 | C7   G7

| sing-er's gon-na sing   a song   and he | wants you all to sing   a-long.   So |

A7 | C7

| let me in-tro-duce to you,   the | one and on-ly Bil-ly Shears,   and |

G7   C7 | G7

| Ser-geant   Pep-per's   Lone - ly Hearts Club Band, | yeah. |

*Segue into "With a Little
Help from My Friends"*

C7

| / / / /   / / / / | / / / /   / / / / ‖

She Loves You

Words and Music by John Lennon and Paul McCartney

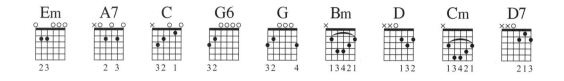

Key of G
Intro
 Moderately

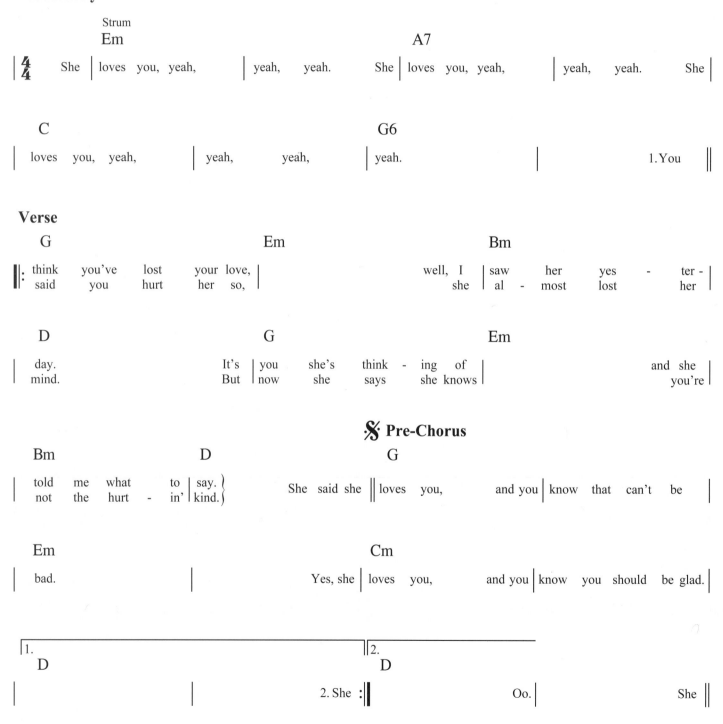

Chorus

Em   A7

| loves you, yeah, | yeah, yeah. She | loves you, yeah, | yeah, yeah. With a |

To Coda ⊕

Cm   N.C.   Strum D7   G

| love like that, you | know you should be glad. | | 3. You ‖

Verse

G   Em   Bm   D

| know it's up to you, | I | think it's on - ly | fair. | |

D.S. al Coda
(take 2nd ending)

G   Em   Bm   D

| Pride can hurt you, too. | A - | pol - o - gize to | her. Be - cause she ‖

⊕ Coda

G   Em   Cm   N.C.   Strum D7

| | | With a | love like that, you | know you should be glad. |

G   Em   Cm   N.C.   D7   N.C.

| | | With a | love like that, you | know you should be ‖

rit.

Outro

G   Em

| glad. | | Yeah, | yeah, yeah. |

C   G6

| Yeah, | yeah, yeah, | yeah. ‖

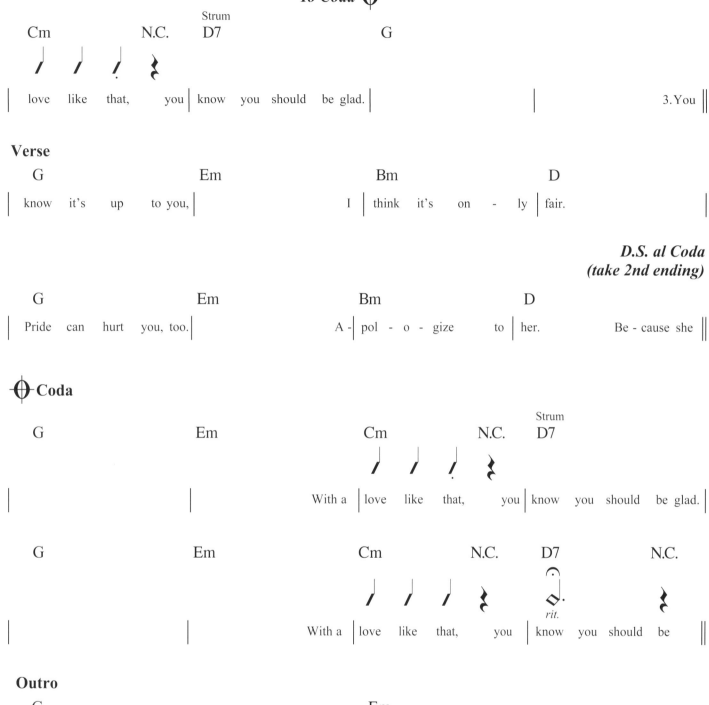
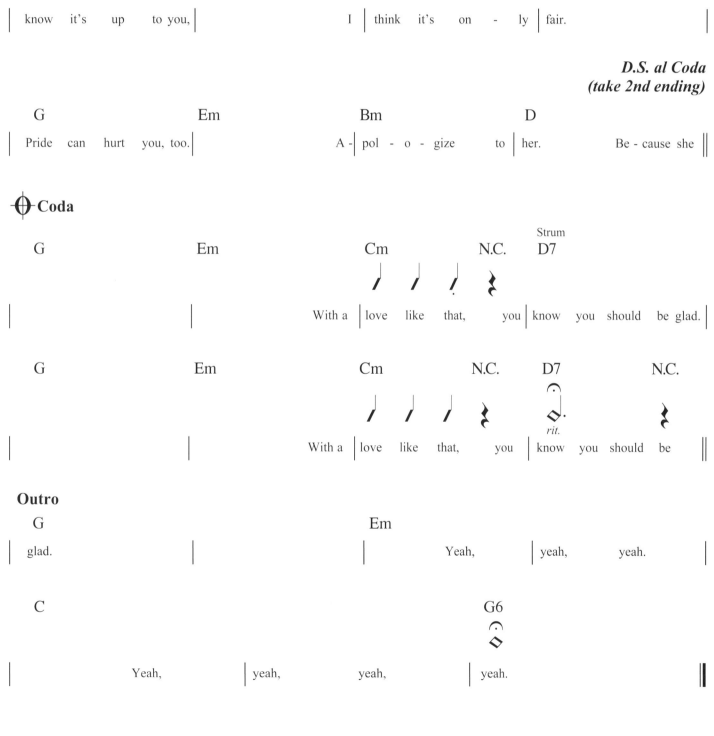

Something

Words and Music by George Harrison

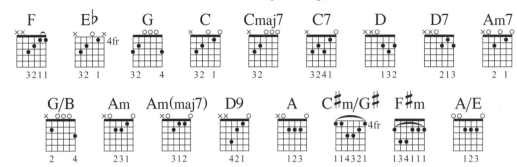

Key of C
Intro
Slow

𝄋 **Verse**

F · · · · · · · · Eb · · · G · · · · · · · · C

1. Some - thing in the way she moves
2. Some - where in her smile she knows
3. *Instrumental*
4. Some - thing in the way she knows

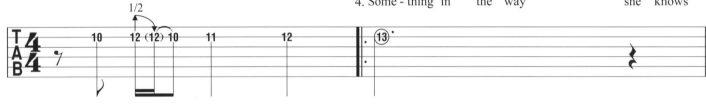

Cmaj7 · · · · · · · C7 · · · · · · · · · · · · · · · · F

at - tracts me like no oth - er lov - er.
that I don't need no oth - er lov - er.
and all I have to do is think of her.

D · · · · · · · · · · · · D7 · · · · · · · · · · G · · · · Am7 · · · G/B

Some - thing in the way she woos me.
Some - thing in the style she shows me.
Some - thing in the things she shows me.

I

4th time, To Coda ⊕

Am · · · · · · · · · · · · · Am(maj7) · · · · · · · · Am7 · · · · · · · D9

don't want to leave her now, you know I be - lieve and how.

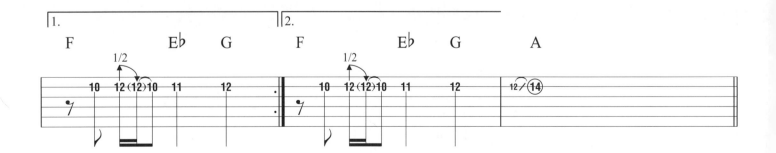

Bridge

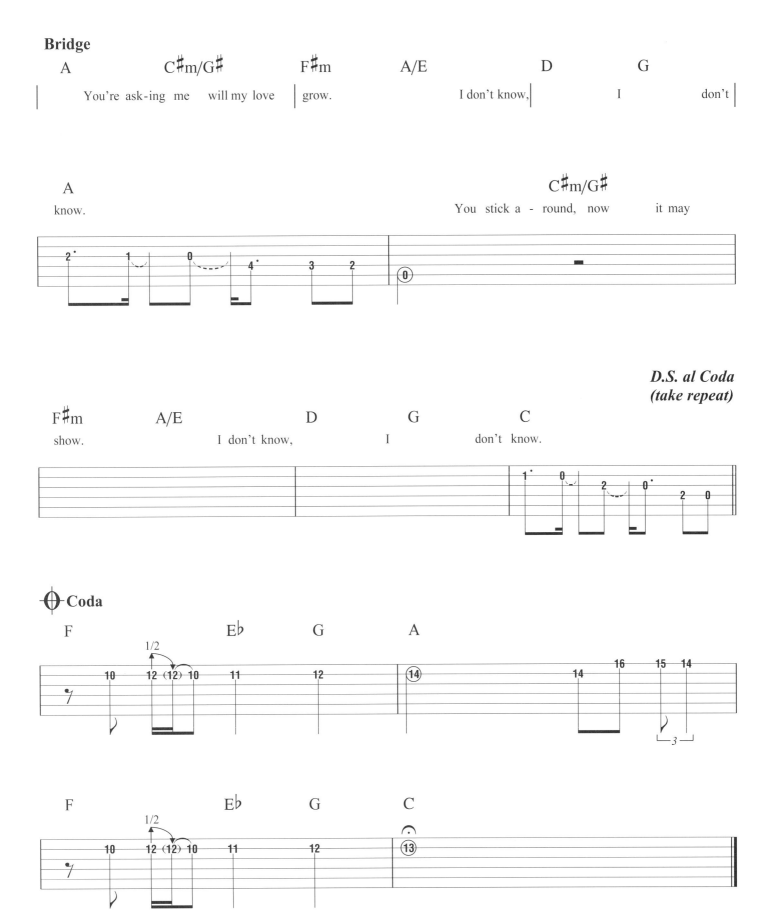

Strawberry Fields Forever

Words and Music by John Lennon and Paul McCartney

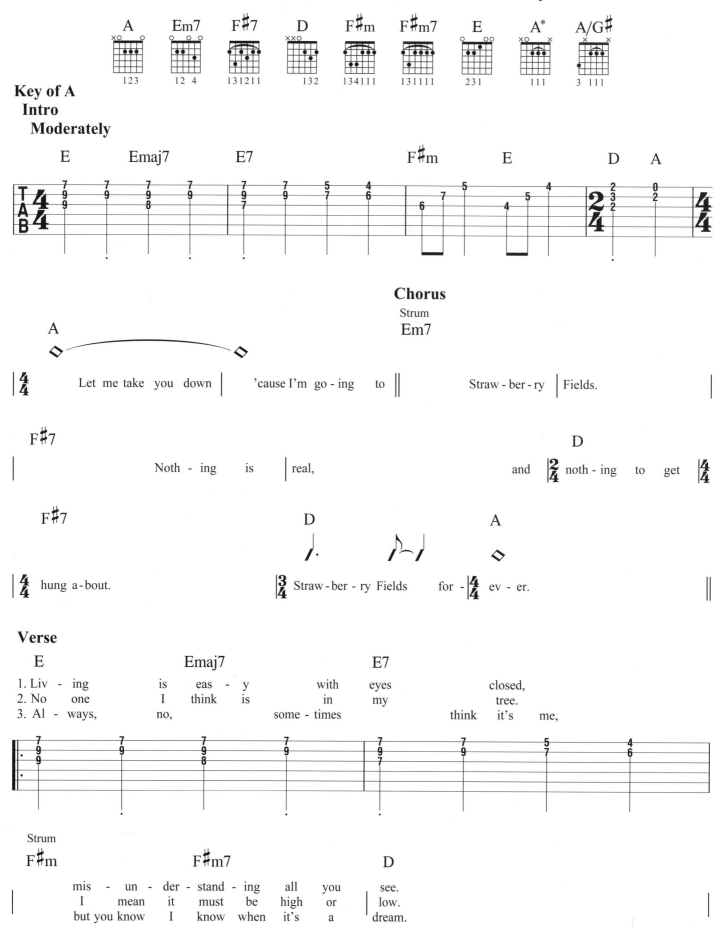

Key of A
Intro
Moderately

A Let me take you down 'cause I'm go - ing to

Chorus
Strum
Em7 Straw - ber - ry Fields.

F#7 Noth - ing is real, and noth - ing to get

F#7 hung a - bout. D Straw - ber - ry Fields A for - ev - er.

Verse

E / Emaj7 / E7
1. Liv - ing is eas - y with eyes closed,
2. No one I think is in my tree.
3. Al - ways, no, some - times think it's me,

Strum
F#m / F#m7 / D
mis - un - der - stand - ing all you see.
I mean it must be high or low.
but you know I know when it's a dream.

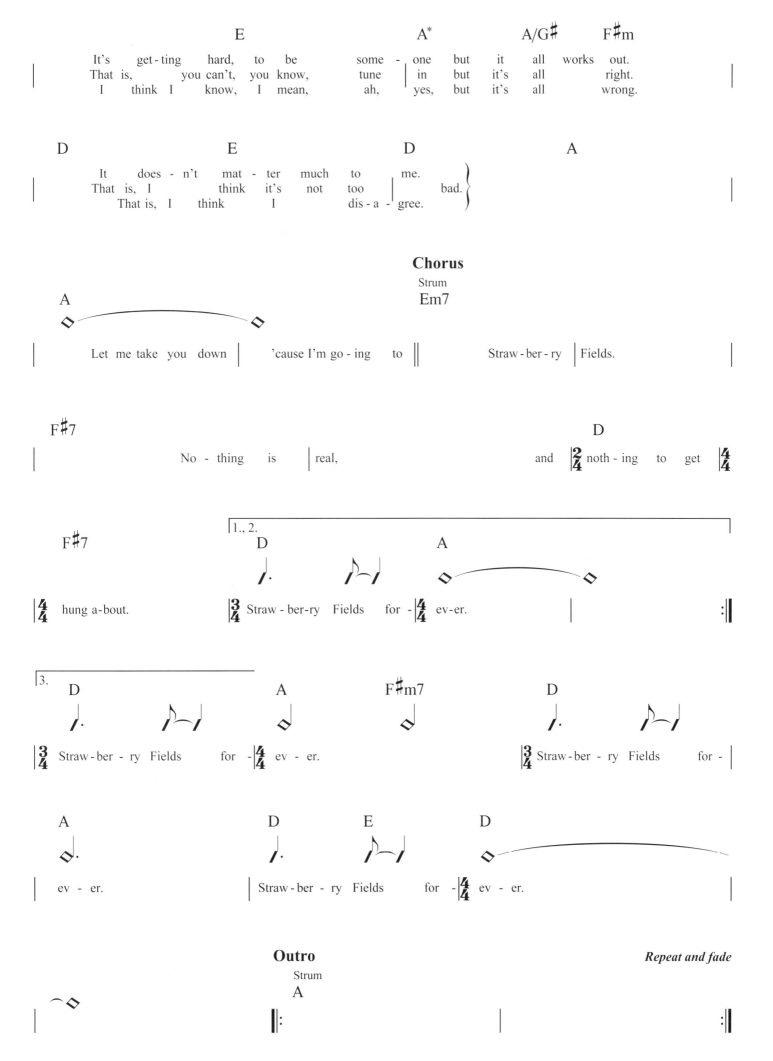

Ticket to Ride

Words and Music by John Lennon and Paul McCartney

Key of A
Intro
Moderately

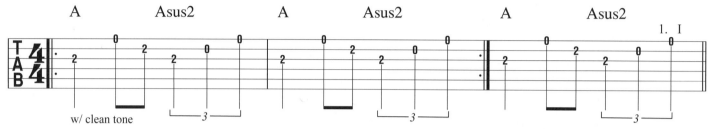

w/ clean tone

Verse

etc.

(3.) think I'm gon-na be sad,   I think it's to-day,   yeah!
(4.) said that liv-ing with me   is bring-in' her down,   yeah!

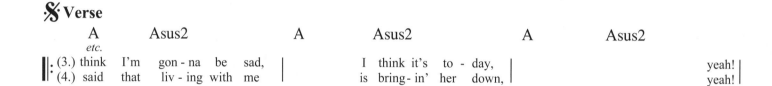

The | girl that's driv-in' me mad   is go-in' a-way.
She would nev-er be free   when I was a-round.

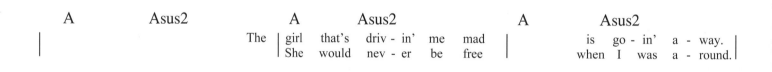

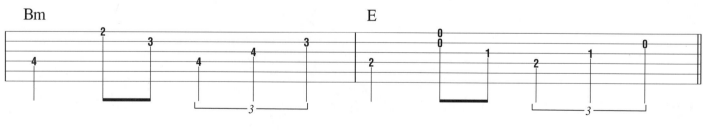

Chorus

She's got a tick-et to ride,   she's got a tick-et to ri-
ride

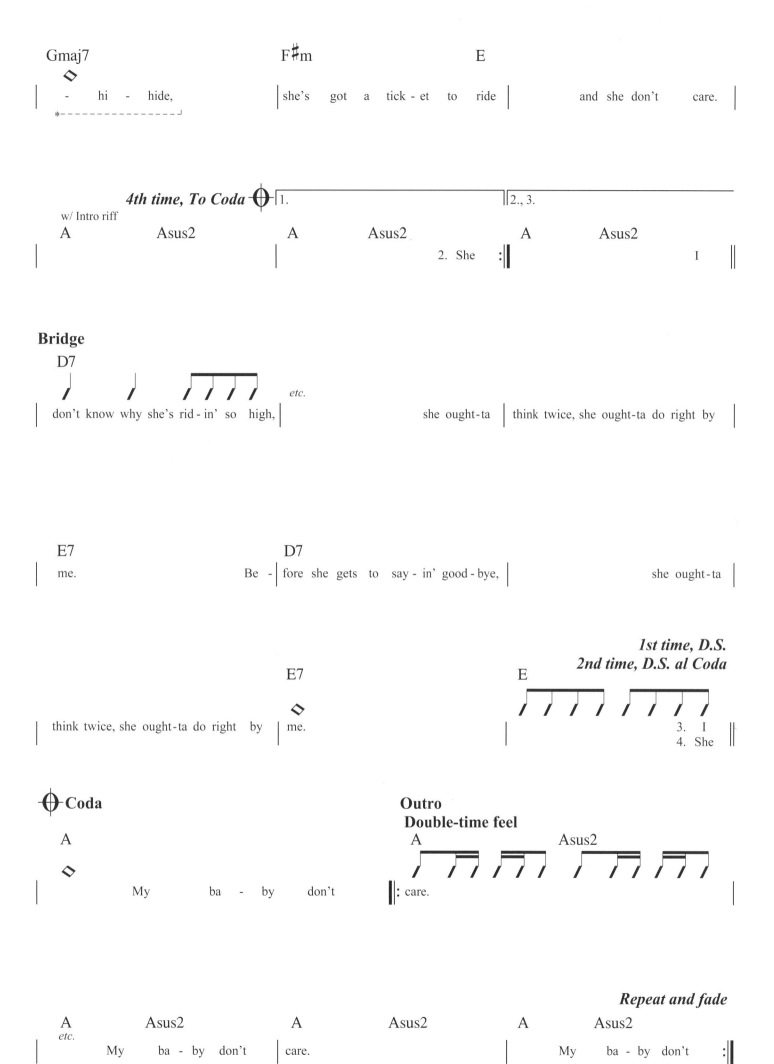

Twist and Shout

Words and Music by Bert Russell and Phil Medley

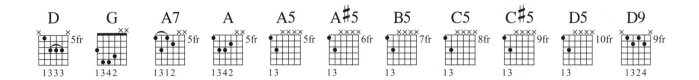

Key of D
Intro
    Moderately

Chorus
w/ Intro riff

D	G	A7		D	G	A7
- by, now. (Shake it up, ba	- by.) Twist and	shout. (Twist and shout.)		Come on, come on, come on, come on,

D	G	A7		D	G	A7
ba - by, now.	Come on and work it all out.		(Work it on out.)	1. Well, work it on out.

(Come on, ba - by.)

Verse

D	G	A7		D	G	A7
(Work it on out.)	You know you look so	good.	(Look so good.)	You know you got me

D	G	A7		D	G	A7
go-in', now.	Just like I knew you would.		(Like I knew you would.)	Well, shake it up ba -

(Got me go - in'.)

𝄋 Chorus

D	G	A7		D	G	A7
- by, now. (Shake it up ba	- by.) Twist and	shout. (Twist and shout.)		Come on, come on, come on, come on,

D	G	A7		D	G	A7
ba-by, now.	Come on and work it on out.		(Work it on out.)	2., 3. You know you twist, lit-tle girl.

(Come on ba - by.)

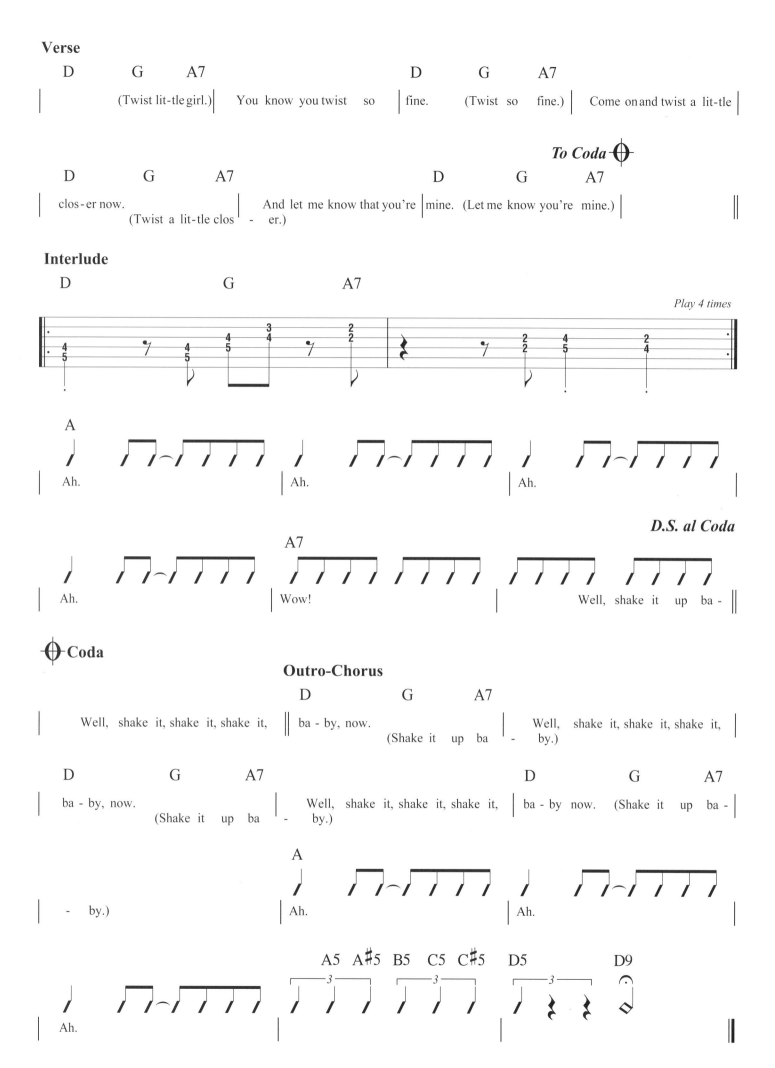

We Can Work It Out

Words and Music by John Lennon and Paul McCartney

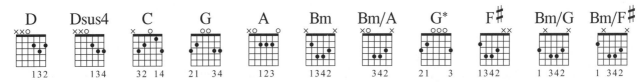

Key of D

Verse

Moderately

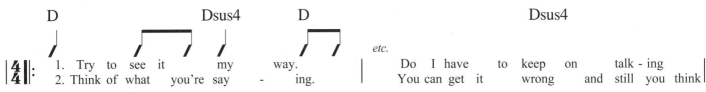

D   Dsus4   D   *etc.*   Dsus4

1. Try to see it   my   way.   Do I have to keep on talk - ing
2. Think of what you're say - ing.   You can get it wrong and still you think

C   D   Dsus4   D

'til I   can't   go   on?   While you see it   your   way,
     that it's al - right.   Think of what I'm say - ing.

Dsus4   C   D

run a risk of know-ing that our   love may soon be gone.
We can work it out and get it straight   or say good - night.

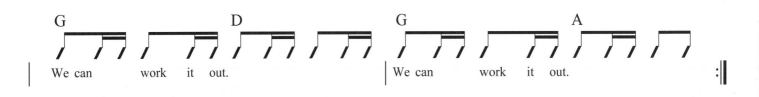

G   D   G   A

We can   work it out.   We can   work it out.

Bridge

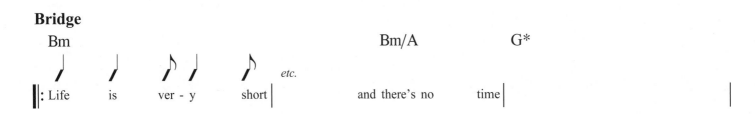

Bm   Bm/A   G*

Life   is   ver - y   short   *etc.*   and there's no   time

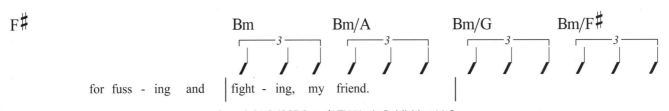

F♯   Bm   Bm/A   Bm/G   Bm/F♯

for fuss - ing and   fight - ing, my friend.

Bm ... Bm/A ... G*

I have al-ways thought that it's a crime,

F#

so I will ask you once a-gain.

Bm ... Bm/A ... Bm/G ... Bm/F#

Verse

D ... Dsus4 ... D ... Dsus4

etc.

3., 4. Try to see it my way. On-ly time will tell if I am

C ... D ... Dsus4 ... D

right or I am wrong. While you see it your way,

Dsus4 ... C ... D

there's a chance that we might fall a-part be-fore too long.

G ... D ... G ... A

We can work it out. We can work it out.

Outro

D

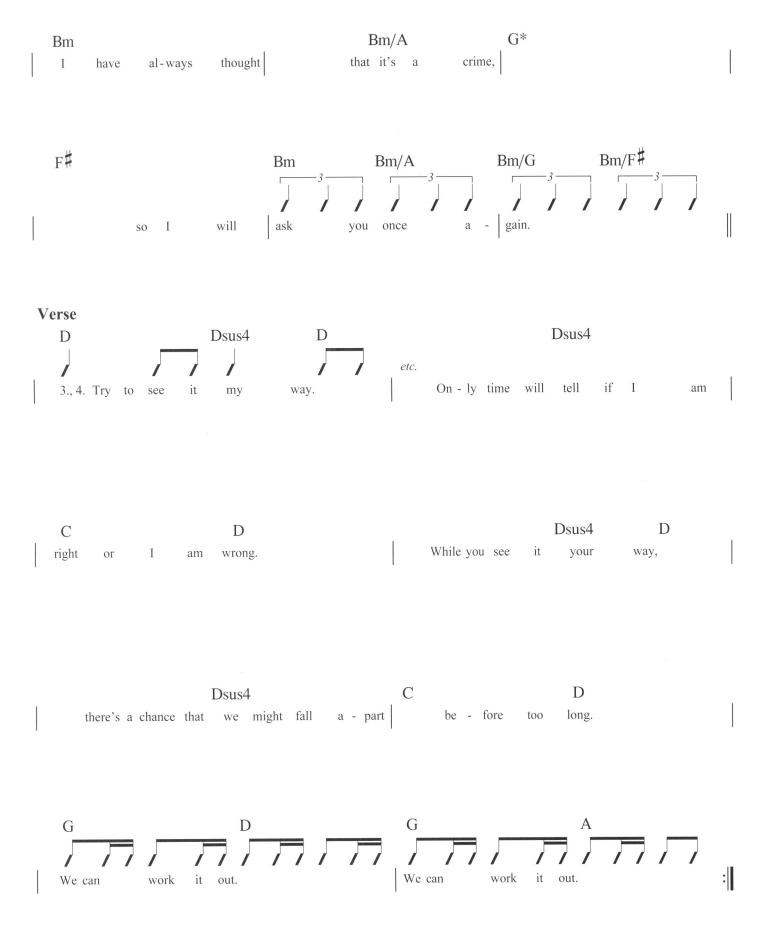

While My Guitar Gently Weeps

Words and Music by George Harrison

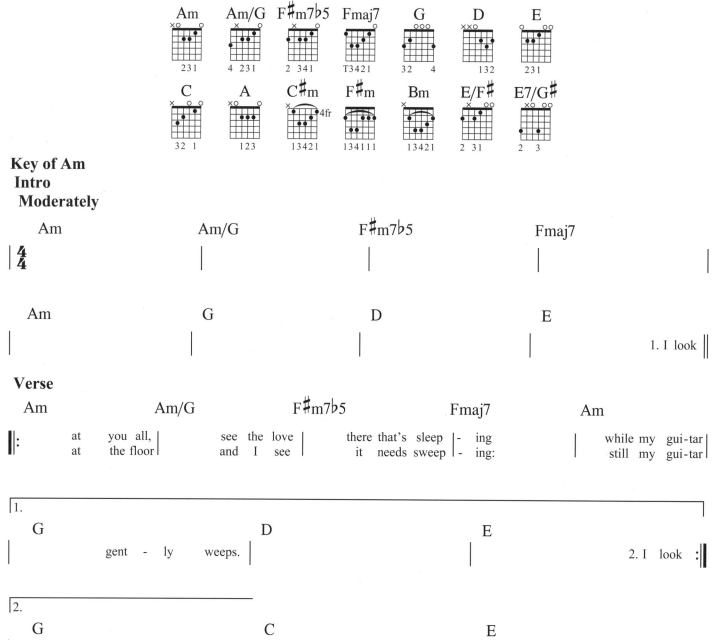

Key of Am
Intro
Moderately

Am   Am/G   F#m7b5   Fmaj7

Am   G   D   E   1. I look

Verse

Am   Am/G   F#m7b5   Fmaj7   Am

at you all,   see the love   there that's sleep|-ing   while my gui-tar
at the floor   and I see   it needs sweep|-ing: still my gui-tar

1.

G   D   E   2. I look

gent - ly weeps.

2.

G   C   E

gent - ly weeps.

Bridge 𝄋

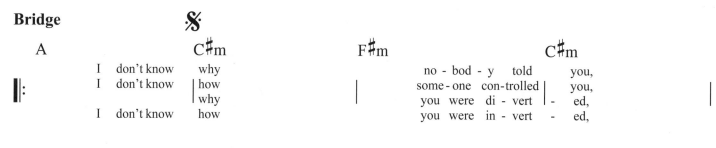

A   C#m   F#m   C#m

I don't know why   no - bod - y told you,
I don't know how   some - one con-trolled|you,
        why   you were di - vert|- ed,
I don't know how   you were in - vert - ed,

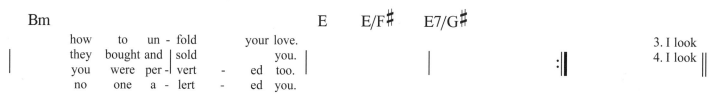

Bm   E   E/F#   E7/G#

how to un - fold your love.   3. I look
they bought and |sold you.   4. I look
you were per - |vert - ed too.
no one a - lert - ed you.

Verse

Am		Am/G		F#m7♭5		Fmaj7	

at the world | and I no | - tice it's turn |- ing |
at you all, | see the love | there that's sleep |- ing |

To Coda ⊕

Am		G		D		E	

while my gui-tar | gent - ly weeps. | | For ev - |
while my gui-tar | gent - ly weeps. | | Look |

Am		Am/G		F#m7♭5		Fmaj7	

- 'ry mis - take | we must sure | - ly be learn |- ing: |

Am		G		C		E	

still my gui-tar | gent - ly weeps. | Yeah. | ‖

Guitar Solo

Am	Am/G	F#m7♭5	Fmaj7	Am	G

D	E	Am	Am/G	F#m7♭5

D.S. al Coda
(take repeat)

Fmaj7	Am	G	C	E	A

I don't know ‖

⊕ **Coda**

Am		Am/G		F#m7♭5		Fmaj7	

at you all. |

Am		G		C		E	

Still my gui-tar | gent - ly weeps. | | ‖

Outro-Guitar Solo

Am		Am/G		F#m7♭5		Fmaj7	

‖: | | | |

Repeat and fade

Am		Am/G		D		E	

| | | :‖

With a Little Help from My Friends

Words and Music by John Lennon and Paul McCartney

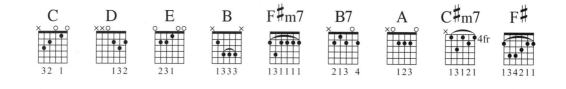

Key of E
Intro
 Moderately

C		D		E		
◇		◇		◇		
4/4 Bil	-	ly		Shears.		

E		B		F#m7			
1. What would you think	if I sang	out of tune?	Would you stand
2. What do I do	when my love	is a - way?	(Does it wor -
3. (Would you be - lieve	in a love	at first sight?)	Yes, I'm cer -

		B7	E		
up and	walk out on me?		
- ry you	to be a - lone?)		
- tain that it	hap-pens all the time.		

B		F#m7		
Lend me your ears	and I'll sing	you a song,	and I'll try
How do I feel	by the end	of the day?	Are you sad
(What do you see	when they turn	out the light?)	I can't tell

	B7	E		
not to sing out of key.	Oh,⟩	I get by
be - cause you're on your own?)	No,⟩	
you but I know it's mine.	Oh,⟩	

Chorus

D		A		E		
with a lit-tle help	from my friends.		Mmm,	I get high

D		A		E		
with a lit-tle help	from my friends.		Mmm,	gon - na try

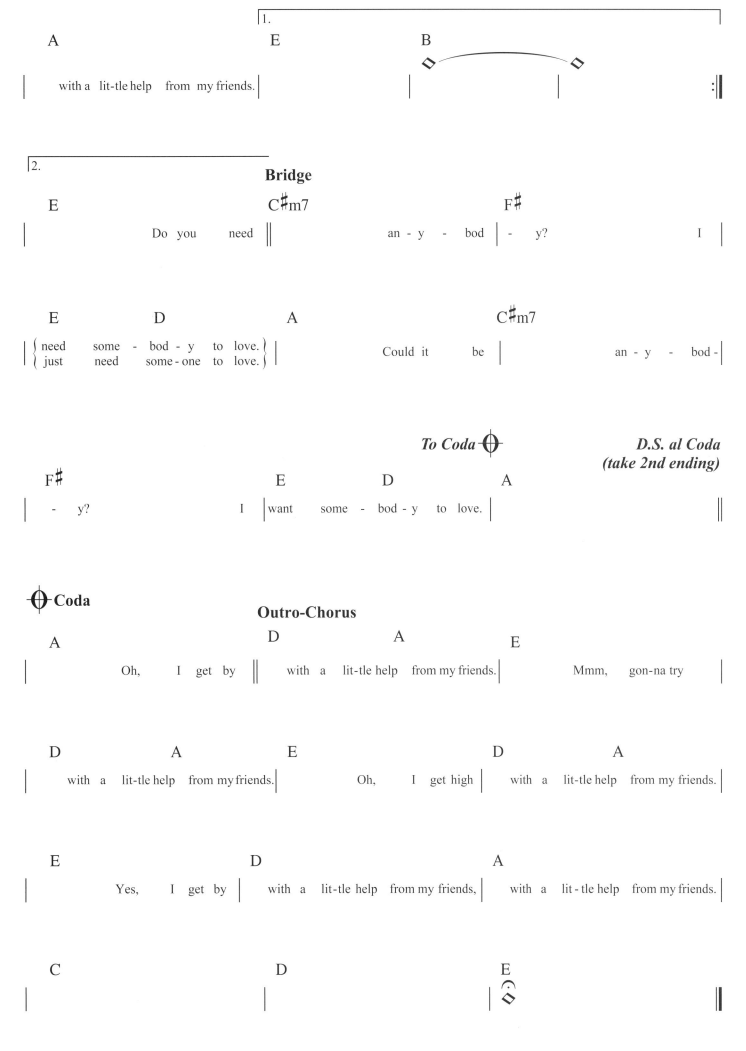

Yellow Submarine

Words and Music by John Lennon and Paul McCartney

 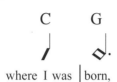 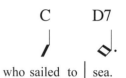

Key of G
Verse
Moderately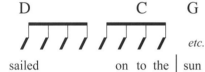

D	C G	Em Am	C D7	G
4/4 1. In the town	where I was born,	lived a man	who sailed to sea.	And he

D	C G	Em Am	C D7	G
etc. told	us of his life	in the land	of sub-ma - rines.	So we

D	C G	Em Am	C D7	G
sailed *etc.*	on to the sun	'til we found	the sea of green.	And we

D	C G	Em Am	C D7
lived	be-neath the waves	in our yel - low	sub-ma - rine.

Chorus

G	D		G
We all live in a	yel-low sub-ma-rine,	yel-low sub-ma-rine,	yel-low sub-ma-rine.

	D		G
etc. We all live in a	yel-low sub-ma-rine,	yel-low sub-ma-rine,	yel-low sub-ma-rine. 2. And our

Verse

D		C	G		Em	Am		C	D7		G

etc.

friends are all on- board, man-y more of them live next door. And the

D		C	G

band be-gins to play.

Chorus

w/ Chorus rhythm

G   D   G

We all live in a yel-low sub-ma-rine, yel-low sub-ma-rine, yel-low sub-ma-rine.

D   G

We all live in a yel-low sub-ma-rine, yel-low sub-ma-rine, yel-low sub-ma-rine.

Interlude

D		C	G		Em	Am		C	D7		G

etc.

Spoken: Full speed | *ahead Mr. Boatswain, full speed ahead.* | *Full speed ahead it is, Sgt.*

D		C	G		Em	Am		C	D7		G

Cut the cable. | *Drop the cable.*   *Aye,* | *sir, aye.*   *Captain, Captain.*   3. As we

Verse

D		C	G		Em	Am		C	D7		G

etc.

live a life of ease, ev-'ry one of us has all we need. Sky of

D		C	G		Em	Am		C	D7		G

blue and sea of green, in our yel - low sub-ma - rine.

Chorus   *Repeat and fade*

w/ Chorus rhythm

G   D   G

‖: We all live in a yel-low sub-ma-rine, yel-low sub-ma-rine, yel-low sub-ma-rine. :‖

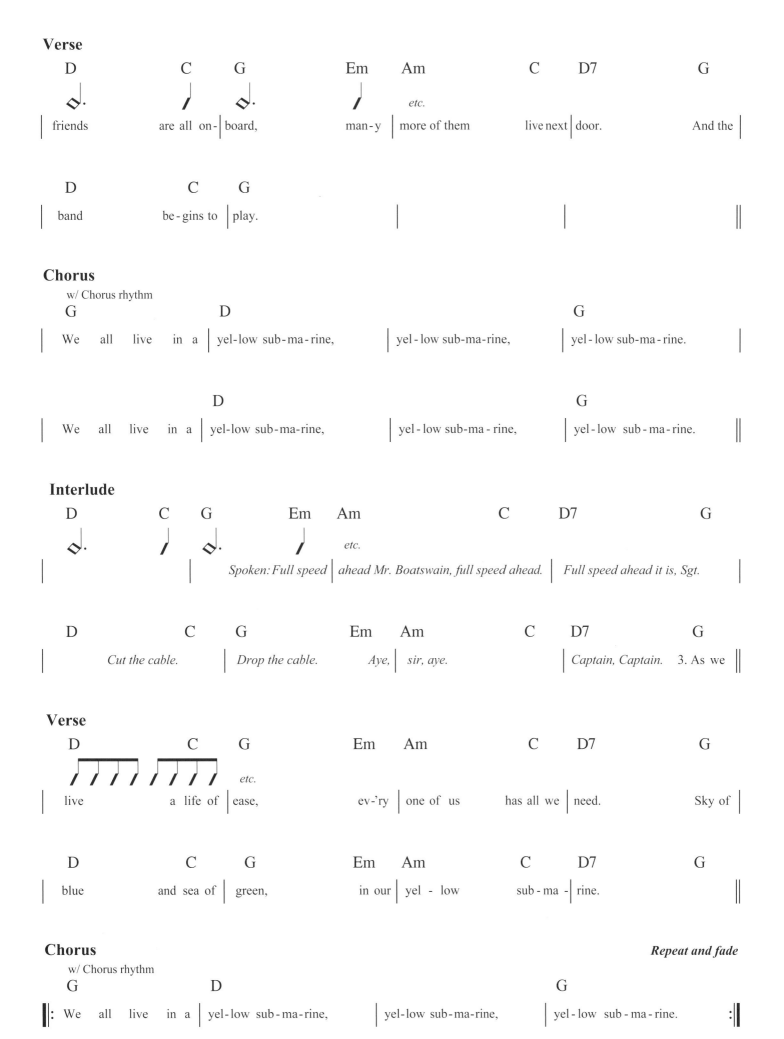

Yesterday

Words and Music by John Lennon and Paul McCartney

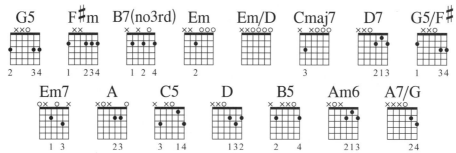

Tune down 1 step:
(low to high) D-G-C-F-A-D

Key of G

Intro

Moderately

G5

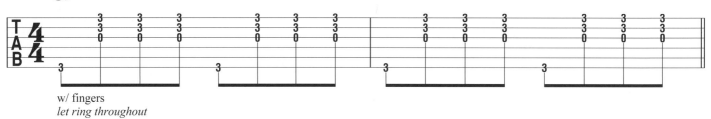

w/ fingers
let ring throughout

Verse

G5 *etc.*	F♯m B7(no3rd)	Em	Em/D
1. Yes - ter - day,	all my trou - bles seemed so	far a - way,	
2. Sud - den - ly,	I'm not half the man I	used to be.	

Cmaj7 D7	G5	G5/F♯ Em7	A
now it looks as though they're	here to stay. Oh,	I be - lieve in	
There's a shad - ow hang - ing o	- ver me. Oh,	yes - ter - day came	

Bridge

C5 G5	F♯m	B7(no3rd)	Em D C5 B5
yes - ter - day.	Why she	had to go, I don't	
sud - den - ly.			

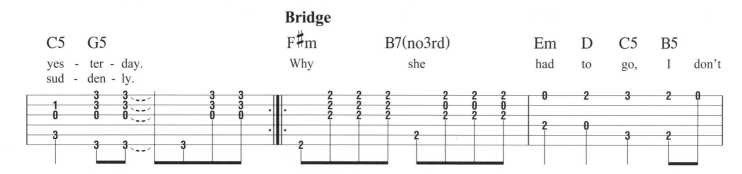

Am6   D7   G5   F♯m   B7(no3rd)

| know, she would - n't say. | | I said |

Em D C5 B5   Am6   D7   G5

| some - thing wrong, now I | long for yes - ter - | day. ||

Verse

 G5   F♯m B7(no3rd)   Em   Em/D

| 3., 4. Yes - ter - day, | love was such an eas - y | game to play. |

Cmaj7   D7   G5   G5/F♯ Em7   A

| Now I need a place to | hide a - way. Oh, | I be - lieve in |

Outro

C5 G5   G5   A7/G   C5 G5

yes - ter - day.   Mm.

RHYTHM TAB LEGEND

Rhythm Tab is a form of notation that adds rhythmic values to the traditional tab staff.

TABLATURE graphically represents the guitar fingerboard. Each horizontal line represents a string, and each number represents a fret. Rhythmic values are shown using ovals, stems, and dots.

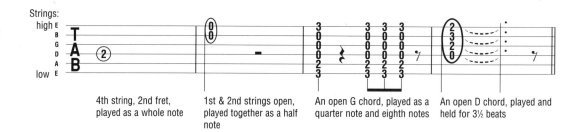

4th string, 2nd fret, played as a whole note

1st & 2nd strings open, played together as a half note

An open G chord, played as a quarter note and eighth notes

An open D chord, played and held for 3½ beats

Definitions for Special Guitar Notation

HALF-STEP BEND: Strike the note and bend up 1/2 step.

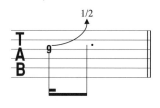

WHOLE-STEP BEND: Strike the note and bend up one step.

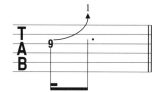

SLIGHT (MICROTONE) BEND: Strike the note and bend up 1/4 step.

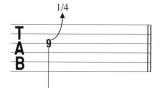

BEND AND RELEASE: Strike the note and bend up as indicated, then release back to the original note. Only the first note is struck.

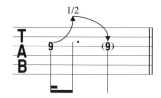

PRE-BEND: Bend the note as indicated, then strike it.

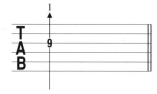

GRACE NOTE PRE-BEND AND RELEASE: Bend the note as indicated. Strike it and release the bend back to the original note.

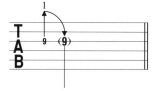

UNISON BEND: Strike the two notes simultaneously and bend the lower note up to the pitch of the higher.

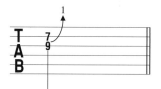

HOLD BEND: While sustaining bent note, strike note on different string.

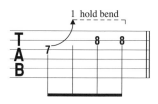

VIBRATO: The string is vibrated by rapidly bending and releasing the note with the fretting hand.

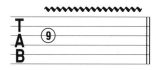

WIDE VIBRATO: The pitch is varied to a greater degree by vibrating with the fretting hand.

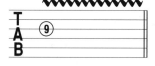

HAMMER-ON: Strike the first (lower) note with one finger, then sound the higher note (on the same string) with another finger by fretting it without picking.

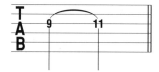

PULL-OFF: Place both fingers on the notes to be sounded. Strike the first note and without picking, pull the finger off to sound the second (lower) note.

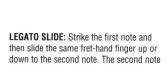

HAMMER FROM NOWHERE: Sound note(s) by hammering with fret hand finger only.

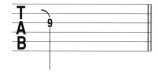

GRACE NOTE SLUR: Strike the note and immediately hammer-on (or pull-off) as indicated.

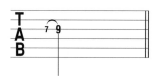

GRACE NOTE SLUR (CLUSTER): Strike the notes and immediately hammer-on (or pull-off) as indicated.

LEGATO SLIDE: Strike the first note and then slide the same fret-hand finger up or down to the second note. The second note is not struck.

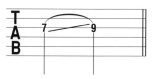

SHIFT SLIDE: Same as legato slide, except the second note is struck.

GRACE NOTE SLIDE: Quickly slide into the note from below or above.

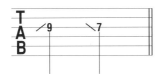

TRILL: Very rapidly alternate between the notes indicated by continuously hammering on and pulling off.

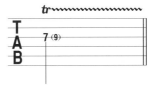

TAPPING: Hammer ("tap") the fret indicated with the pick-hand index or middle finger and pull off to the note fretted by the fret hand.

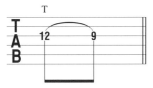

NATURAL HARMONIC: Strike the note while the fret-hand lightly touches the string directly over the fret indicated.

PINCH HARMONIC: The note is fretted normally and a harmonic is produced by adding the edge of the thumb or the tip of the index finger of the pick hand to the normal pick attack.

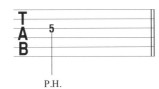

HARP HARMONIC: The note is fretted normally and a harmonic is produced by gently resting the pick hand's index finger directly above the indicated fret (in parentheses) while the pick hand's thumb or pick assists by plucking the appropriate string.

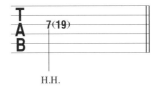

PICK SCRAPE: The edge of the pick is rubbed down (or up) the string, producing a scratchy sound.

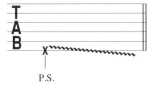

MUFFLED STRINGS: A percussive sound is produced by laying the fret hand across the string(s) without depressing, and striking them with the pick hand.

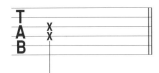

PALM MUTING: The note is partially muted by the pick hand lightly touching the string(s) just before the bridge.

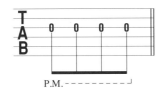

RAKE: Drag the pick across the strings indicated with a single motion.

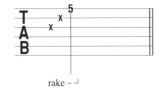

TREMOLO PICKING: The note is picked as rapidly and continuously as possible.

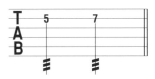

ARPEGGIATE: Play the notes of the chord indicated by quickly rolling them from bottom to top.

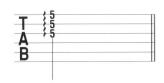

VIBRATO BAR DIVE AND RETURN: The pitch of the note or chord is dropped a specified number of steps (in rhythm), then returned to the original pitch.

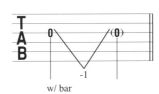

VIBRATO BAR SCOOP: Depress the bar just before striking the note, then quickly release the bar.

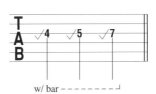

VIBRATO BAR DIP: Strike the note and then immediately drop a specified number of steps, then release back to the original pitch.

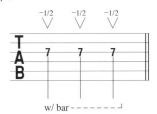

Additional Musical Definitions

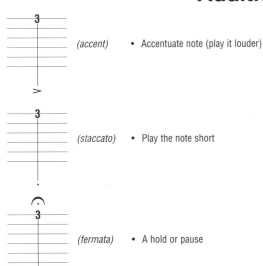

(accent) • Accentuate note (play it louder)

(staccato) • Play the note short

(fermata) • A hold or pause

⊓ • Downstroke

∨ • Upstroke

• Repeat measures between signs

NOTE: Tablature numbers in parentheses are used when:
• The note is sustained, but a new articulation begins (such as a hammer-on, pull-off, slide, or bend), or
• A bend is released.
• A note sustains while crossing from one staff to another.

FIRST 50

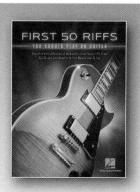

Books in the First 50 series contain easy to intermediate arrangements for must-know songs. Each arrangement is simple and streamlined, yet still captures the essence of the tune.

First 50 Bluegrass Solos You Should Play on Guitar
I Am a Man of Constant Sorrow • Long Journey Home • Molly and Tenbrooks • Old Joe Clark • Rocky Top • Salty Dog Blues • and more!
00298574 Solo Guitar......................................$14.99

First 50 Blues Songs You Should Play on Guitar
All Your Love (I Miss Loving) • Bad to the Bone • Born Under a Bad Sign • Dust My Broom • Hoodoo Man Blues • Little Red Rooster • Love Struck Baby • Pride and Joy • Smoking Gun • Still Got the Blues • The Thrill Is Gone • You Shook Me • and many more.
00235790 Guitar...$14.99

First 50 Blues Turnarounds You Should Play on Guitar
You'll learn cool turnarounds in the styles of these jazz legends: John Lee Hooker, Robert Johnson, Joe Pass, Jimmy Rogers, Hubert Sumlin, Stevie Ray Vaughan, T-Bone Walker, Muddy Waters, and more!
00277469 Guitar...$14.99

First 50 Chords You Should Play on Guitar
American Pie • Back in Black • Brown Eyed Girl • Landslide • Let It Be • Riptide • Summer of '69 • Take Me Home, Country Roads • Won't Get Fooled Again • You've Got a Friend • and more.
00300255 Guitar...$12.99

First 50 Classical Pieces You Should Play on Guitar
This collection includes compositions by J.S. Bach, Augustin Barrios, Matteo Carcassi, Domenico Scarlatti, Fernando Sor, Francisco Tárrega, Robert de Visée, Antonio Vivaldi and many more.
00155414 Solo Guitar $14.99

First 50 Folk Songs You Should Play on Guitar
Amazing Grace • Down by the Riverside • Home on the Range • I've Been Working on the Railroad • Kumbaya • Man of Constant Sorrow • Oh! Susanna • This Little Light of Mine • When the Saints Go Marching In • The Yellow Rose of Texas • and more.
00235868 Guitar...$14.99

First 50 Jazz Standards You Should Play on Guitar
All the Things You Are • Body and Soul • Don't Get Around Much Anymore • Fly Me to the Moon (In Other Words) • The Girl from Ipanema (Garota De Ipanema) • I Got Rhythm • Laura • Misty • Night and Day • Satin
00198594 Solo Guitar $14.99

First 50 Kids' Songs You Should Play on Guitar
Do-Re-Mi • Hakuna Matata • Let It Go • My Favorite Things • Puff the Magic Dragon • Take Me Out to the Ball Game • Won't You Be My Neighbor? (It's a Beautiful Day in the Neighborhood) • and more.
00300500 Guitar...$14.99

First 50 Licks You Should Play on Guitar
Licks presented include the styles of legendary guitarists like Eric Clapton, Buddy Guy, Jimi Hendrix, B.B. King, Randy Rhoads, Carlos Santana, Stevie Ray Vaughan and many more.
00278875 Book/Online Audio $14.99

First 50 Riffs You Should Play on Guitar
All Right Now • Back in Black • Barracuda • Carry on Wayward Son • Crazy Train • La Grange • Layla • Seven Nation Army • Smoke on the Water • Sunday Bloody Sunday • Sunshine of Your Love • Sweet Home Alabama • Working Man • and more!
00277366 Guitar...$12.99

First 50 Rock Songs You Should Play on Electric Guitar
All Along the Watchtower • Beat It • Brown Eyed Girl • Cocaine • Detroit Rock City • Hallelujah • (I Can't Get No) Satisfaction • Oh, Pretty Woman • Pride and Joy • Seven Nation Army • Should I Stay or Should I Go • Smells like Teen Spirit • Smoke on the Water • When I Come Around • You Really Got Me • and more.
00131159 Guitar...$14.99

First 50 Songs You Should Fingerpick on Guitar
Annie's Song • Blackbird • The Boxer • Classical Gas • Dust in the Wind • Fire and Rain • Greensleeves • Road Trippin' • Shape of My Heart • Tears in Heaven • Time in a Bottle • Vincent (Starry Starry Night) • and more.
00149269 Solo Guitar $14.99

First 50 Songs You Should Play on 12-String Guitar
California Dreamin' • Closer to the Heart • Free Fallin' • Give a Little Bit • Hotel California • Leaving on a Jet Plane • Life by the Drop • Over the Hills and Far Away • Solsbury Hill • Space Oddity • Wish You Were Here • You Wear It Well • and more!
00287559 Guitar...$14.99

First 50 Songs You Should Play on Acoustic Guitar
Against the Wind • Boulevard of Broken Dreams • Champagne Supernova • Every Rose Has Its Thorn • Fast Car • Free Fallin' • Layla • Let Her Go • Mean • One • Ring of Fire • Signs • Stairway to Heaven • Trouble • Wagon Wheel • Yellow • Yesterday • and more.
00131209 Guitar $14.99

First 50 Songs You Should Play on Bass
Blister in the Sun • I Got You (I Feel Good) • Livin' on a Prayer • Low Rider • Money • Monkey Wrench • My Generation • Roxanne • Should I Stay or Should I Go • Uptown Funk • What's Going On • With or Without You • Yellow • and more!
00149189 Bass Tab Arrangements...............$14.99

First 50 Songs You Should Play on Solo Guitar
Africa • All of Me • Blue Skies • California Dreamin' • Change the World • Crazy • Dream a Little Dream of Me • Every Breath You Take • Hallelujah • Wonderful Tonight • Yesterday • You Raise Me Up • Your Song • and more.
00288843 Guitar...$14.99

First 50 Songs You Should Strum on Guitar
American Pie • Blowin' in the Wind • Daughter • Hey, Soul Sister • Home • I Will Wait • Losing My Religion • Mrs. Robinson • No Woman No Cry • Peaceful Easy Feeling • Rocky Mountain High • Sweet Caroline • Teardrops on My Guitar • Wonderful Tonight • and more.
00148996 Guitar...$14.99

Prices, contents and availability subject to change without notice.

www.halleonard.com

0220
014

DELUXE GUITAR PLAY-ALONG

AUDIO ACCESS INCLUDED 🔊

The Deluxe Guitar Play-Along series will help you play songs faster than ever before! Accurate, easy-to-read guitar tab and professional, customizable audio for 15 songs. The interactive, online audio interface includes tempo/pitch control, looping, buttons to turn instruments on or off, and guitar tab with follow-along marker. The price of each book includes access to audio tracks online using the unique code inside. The tracks can also be downloaded and played offline. Now including PLAYBACK+, a multi-functional audio player that allows you to slow down audio, change pitch, set loop points, and pan left or right – available exclusively from Hal Leonard.

1. TOP ROCK HITS
Basket Case • Black Hole Sun • Come As You Are • Do I Wanna Know? • Gold on the Ceiling • Heaven • How You Remind Me • Kryptonite • No One Knows • Plush • The Pretender • Seven Nation Army • Smooth • Under the Bridge • Yellow Ledbetter.

00244758 Book/Online Audio............ $19.99

2. REALLY EASY SONGS
All the Small Things • Brain Stew • Californication • Free Fallin' • Helter Skelter • Hey Joe • Highway to Hell • Hurt (Quiet) • I Love Rock 'N Roll • Island in the Sun • Knockin' on Heaven's Door • La Bamba • Oh, Pretty Woman • Should I Stay or Should I Go • Smells Like Teen Spirit.

00244877 Book/Online Audio............ $19.99

3. ACOUSTIC SONGS
All Apologies • Banana Pancakes • Crash Into Me • Good Riddance (Time of Your Life) • Hallelujah • Hey There Delilah • Ho Hey • I Will Wait • I'm Yours • Iris • More Than Words • No Such Thing • Photograph • What I Got • Wonderwall.

00244709 Book/Online Audio............ $19.99

4. THE BEATLES
All My Loving • And I Love Her • Back in the U.S.S.R. • Don't Let Me Down • Get Back • A Hard Day's Night • Here Comes the Sun • I Will • In My Life • Let It Be • Michelle • Paperback Writer • Revolution • While My Guitar Gently Weeps • Yesterday.

00244968 Book/Online Audio............ $19.99

5. BLUES STANDARDS
Baby, What You Want Me to Do • Crosscut Saw • Double Trouble • Every Day I Have the Blues • Going Down • I'm Tore Down • I'm Your Hoochie Coochie Man • If You Love Me Like You Say • Just Your Fool • Killing Floor • Let Me Love You Baby • Messin' with the Kid • Pride and Joy • (They Call It) Stormy Monday (Stormy Monday Blues) • Sweet Home Chicago.

00245090 Book/Online Audio............ $19.99

6. RED HOT CHILI PEPPERS
The Adventures of Rain Dance Maggie • Breaking the Girl • Can't Stop • Dani California • Dark Necessities • Give It Away • My Friends • Otherside • Road Trippin' • Scar Tissue • Snow (Hey Oh) • Suck My Kiss • Tell Me Baby • Under the Bridge • The Zephyr Song.

00245089 Book/Online Audio............ $19.99

7. CLASSIC ROCK
Baba O'Riley • Born to Be Wild • Comfortably Numb • Dream On • Fortunate Son • Heartbreaker • Hotel California • Jet Airliner • More Than a Feeling • Old Time Rock & Roll • Rhiannon • Runnin' Down a Dream • Start Me Up • Sultans of Swing • Sweet Home Alabama.

00248381 Book/Online Audio............ $19.99

8. OZZY OSBOURNE
Bark at the Moon • Close My Eyes Forever • Crazy Train • Dreamer • Goodbye to Romance • I Don't Know • I Don't Wanna Stop • Mama, I'm Coming Home • Miracle Man • Mr. Crowley • No More Tears • Over the Mountain • Perry Mason • Rock 'N Roll Rebel • Shot in the Dark.

00248413 Book/Online Audio............ $19.99

9. ED SHEERAN
The A Team • All of the Stars • Castle on the Hill • Don't • Drunk • Galway Girl • Give Me Love • How Would You Feel (Paean) • I See Fire • Lego House • Make It Rain • Perfect • Photograph • Shape of You • Thinking Out Loud.

00248439 Book/Online Audio............ $19.99

10. THREE-CHORD SONGS
Ain't No Sunshine • All Along the Watchtower • Bad Moon Rising • Beverly Hills • Can't You See • Evil Ways • I Still Haven't Found What I'm Looking For • The Joker • Just the Way You Are • Ring of Fire • Stir It Up • Twist and Shout • What I Got • What's Up • Wicked Game.

00278488 Book/Online Audio............ $19.99

11. FOUR CHORD SONGS
Chasing Cars • Cruise • Demons • Hand in My Pocket • Hey, Soul Sister • Hey Ya! • If I Had $1,000,000 • Riptide • Rude • Save Tonight • Steal My Girl • Steal My Kisses • 3 AM • Toes • Zombie.

00287263 Book/Online Audio............ $19.99

12. KISS
Christine Sixteen • Cold Gin • Detroit Rock City • Deuce • Firehouse • God of Thunder • Heaven's on Fire • I Stole Your Love • I Was Made for Lovin' You • Lick It Up • Love Gun • Rock and Roll All Nite • Shock Me • Shout It Out Loud • Strutter.

00288989 Book/Online Audio............ $19.99

13. CHRISTMAS CLASSICS
Angels We Have Heard on High • Away in a Manger • Deck the Hall • The First Noel • Go, Tell It on the Mountain • God Rest Ye Merry, Gentlemen • Hark! the Herald Angels Sing • It Came upon the Midnight Clear • Jingle Bells • Joy to the World • O Come, All Ye Faithful • O Holy Night • O Little Town of Bethlehem • Silent Night • We Three Kings of Orient Are.

00294776 Book/Online Audio............ $19.99

14. NEIL YOUNG
Cinnamon Girl • Comes a Time • Cowgirl in the Sand • Down by the River • Harvest Moon • Heart of Gold • Helpless • Hey Hey, My My (Into the Black) • Like a Hurricane • The Needle and the Damage Done • Ohio • Old Man • Only Love Can Break Your Heart • Rockin' in the Free World • Southern Man.

00322911 Book/Online Audio............ $24.99

HAL•LEONARD®
www.halleonard.com

Prices, contents, and availability
subject to change without notice.

EASY GUITAR WITH NOTES & TAB

This series features simplified arrangements with notes, tab, chord charts, and strum and pick patterns.

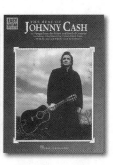

MIXED FOLIOS

00702287	Acoustic	$16.99
00702002	Acoustic Rock Hits for Easy Guitar	$15.99
00702166	All-Time Best Guitar Collection	$19.99
00702232	Best Acoustic Songs for Easy Guitar	$14.99
00119835	Best Children's Songs	$16.99
00702233	Best Hard Rock Songs	$15.99
00703055	The Big Book of Nursery Rhymes & Children's Songs	$16.99
00322179	The Big Easy Book of Classic Rock Guitar	$24.95
00698978	Big Christmas Collection	$17.99
00702394	Bluegrass Songs for Easy Guitar	$12.99
00289632	Bohemian Rhapsody	$17.99
00703387	Celtic Classics	$14.99
00224808	Chart Hits of 2016-2017	$14.99
00267383	Chart Hits of 2017-2018	$14.99
00702149	Children's Christian Songbook	$9.99
00702028	Christmas Classics	$8.99
00101779	Christmas Guitar	$14.99
00702185	Christmas Hits	$10.99
00702141	Classic Rock	$8.95
00159642	Classical Melodies	$12.99
00253933	Disney/Pixar's Coco	$16.99
00702203	CMT's 100 Greatest Country Songs	$29.99

00702283	The Contemporary Christian Collection	$16.99
00196954	Contemporary Disney	$16.99
00702239	Country Classics for Easy Guitar	$22.99
00702257	Easy Acoustic Guitar Songs	$14.99
00702280	Easy Guitar Tab White Pages	$29.99
00702041	Favorite Hymns for Easy Guitar	$10.99
00222701	Folk Pop Songs	$14.99
00140841	4-Chord Hymns for Guitar	$9.99
00702281	4 Chord Rock	$10.99
00126894	Frozen	$14.99
00702286	Glee	$16.99
00699374	Gospel Favorites	$16.99
00702160	The Great American Country Songbook	$16.99
00702050	Great Classical Themes for Easy Guitar	$8.99
00702116	Greatest Hymns for Guitar	$10.99
00275088	The Greatest Showman	$17.99
00148030	Halloween Guitar Songs	$14.99
00702273	Irish Songs	$12.99
00192503	Jazz Classics for Easy Guitar	$14.99
00702275	Jazz Favorites for Easy Guitar	$15.99
00702274	Jazz Standards for Easy Guitar	$16.99
00702162	Jumbo Easy Guitar Songbook	$19.99
00232285	La La Land	$16.99
00702258	Legends of Rock	$14.99
00702189	MTV's 100 Greatest Pop Songs	$24.95

00702272	1950s Rock	$15.99
00702271	1960s Rock	$15.99
00702270	1970s Rock	$16.99
00702269	1980s Rock	$15.99
00702268	1990s Rock	$19.99
00109725	Once	$14.99
00702187	Selections from O Brother Where Art Thou?	$17.99
00702178	100 Songs for Kids	$14.99
00702515	Pirates of the Caribbean	$14.99
00702125	Praise and Worship for Guitar	$10.99
00287930	Songs from *A Star Is Born, The Greatest Showman, La La Land,* and More Movie Musicals	$16.99
00702285	Southern Rock Hits	$12.99
00156420	Star Wars Music	$14.99
00121535	30 Easy Celtic Guitar Solos	$15.99
00702220	Today's Country Hits	$12.99
00121900	Today's Women of Pop & Rock	$14.99
00244654	Top Hits of 2017	$14.99
00283786	Top Hits of 2018	$14.99
00702294	Top Worship Hits	$15.99
00702255	VH1's 100 Greatest Hard Rock Songs	$27.99
00702175	VH1's 100 Greatest Songs of Rock and Roll	$24.99
00702253	Wicked	$12.99

ARTIST COLLECTIONS

00702267	AC/DC for Easy Guitar	$15.99
00702598	Adele for Easy Guitar	$15.99
00156221	Adele – 25	$16.99
00702040	Best of the Allman Brothers	$16.99
00702865	J.S. Bach for Easy Guitar	$14.99
00702169	Best of The Beach Boys	$12.99
00702292	The Beatles — 1	$19.99
00125796	Best of Chuck Berry	$15.99
00702201	The Essential Black Sabbath	$12.95
02501615	Zac Brown Band — The Foundation	$16.99
02501621	Zac Brown Band — You Get What You Give	$16.99
00702043	Best of Johnny Cash	$16.99
00702090	Eric Clapton's Best	$12.99
00702086	Eric Clapton — from the Album Unplugged	$15.99
00702202	The Essential Eric Clapton	$14.99
00702250	blink-182 — Greatest Hits	$15.99
00702053	Best of Patsy Cline	$15.99
00222697	Very Best of Coldplay – 2nd Edition	$14.99
00702229	The Very Best of Creedence Clearwater Revival	$15.99
00702145	Best of Jim Croce	$15.99
00702278	Crosby, Stills & Nash	$12.99
14042809	Bob Dylan	$14.99
00702276	Fleetwood Mac — Easy Guitar Collection	$14.99
00139462	The Very Best of Grateful Dead	$15.99
00702136	Best of Merle Haggard	$14.99
00702227	Jimi Hendrix — Smash Hits	$16.99
00702288	Best of Hillsong United	$12.99
00702236	Best of Antonio Carlos Jobim	$14.99
00702245	Elton John — Greatest Hits 1970–2002	$17.99

00129855	Jack Johnson	$16.99
00702204	Robert Johnson	$10.99
00702234	Selections from Toby Keith — 35 Biggest Hits	$12.95
00702003	Kiss	$12.99
00702216	Lynyrd Skynyrd	$15.99
00702182	The Essential Bob Marley	$14.99
00146081	Maroon 5	$14.99
00121925	Bruno Mars – Unorthodox Jukebox	$12.99
00702248	Paul McCartney — All the Best	$14.99
00702129	Songs of Sarah McLachlan	$12.95
00125484	The Best of MercyMe	$12.99
02501316	Metallica — Death Magnetic	$19.99
00702209	Steve Miller Band — Young Hearts (Greatest Hits)	$12.95
00124167	Jason Mraz	$15.99
00702096	Best of Nirvana	$15.99
00702211	The Offspring — Greatest Hits	$12.95
00138026	One Direction	$14.99
00702030	Best of Roy Orbison	$15.99
00702144	Best of Ozzy Osbourne	$14.99
00702279	Tom Petty	$12.99
00102911	Pink Floyd	$16.99
00702139	Elvis Country Favorites	$16.99
00702293	The Very Best of Prince	$15.99
00699415	Best of Queen for Guitar	$15.99
00109279	Best of R.E.M.	$14.99
00702208	Red Hot Chili Peppers — Greatest Hits	$15.99
00198960	The Rolling Stones	$16.99
00174793	The Very Best of Santana	$14.99
00702196	Best of Bob Seger	$12.95
00146046	Ed Sheeran	$14.99
00702252	Frank Sinatra — Nothing But the Best	$12.99

00702010	Best of Rod Stewart	$16.99
00702049	Best of George Strait	$14.99
00702259	Taylor Swift for Easy Guitar	$15.99
00254499	Taylor Swift – Easy Guitar Anthology	$19.99
00702260	Taylor Swift — Fearless	$14.99
00139727	Taylor Swift — 1989	$17.99
00115960	Taylor Swift — Red	$16.99
00253667	Taylor Swift — Reputation	$17.99
00702290	Taylor Swift — Speak Now	$16.99
00232849	Chris Tomlin Collection – 2nd Edition	$14.99
00702226	Chris Tomlin — See the Morning	$12.95
00148643	Train	$14.99
00702427	U2 — 18 Singles	$16.99
00702108	Best of Stevie Ray Vaughan	$16.99
00279005	The Who	$14.99
00702123	Best of Hank Williams	$14.99
00194548	Best of John Williams	$14.99
00702111	Stevie Wonder — Guitar Collection	$9.95
00702228	Neil Young — Greatest Hits	$15.99
00119133	Neil Young — Harvest	$14.99

Prices, contents and availability subject to change without notice.

Visit Hal Leonard online at **halleonard.com**

0819
306

MORE TIMELESS COLLECTIONS FROM

THE BEATLES

presented by

HAL•LEONARD®

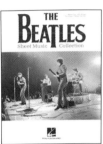

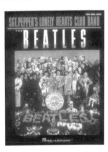

HAL•LEONARD®

Visit our web site at www.halleonard.com for complete songlists and a listing of all products available.

Prices, contents and availability subject to change without notice.

The Beatles Complete
Volume 1
103 songs from A-I: All You Need Is Love • Back in the U.S.S.R. • Blackbird • Come Together • Day Tripper • Eleanor Rigby • The Fool on the Hill • Hello, Goodbye • I Want to Hold Your Hand • and more.
00356240 Piano/Vocal/Guitar $32.50

Volume 2
104 songs from I-Y: In My Life • Let It Be • Lucy in the Sky with Diamonds • Norwegian Wood • Paperback Writer • Twist and Shout • When I'm Sixty Four • With a Little Help from My Friends • Yesterday • and more.
00356241 Piano/Vocal/Guitar $32.50

The Beatles – 1
27 British and American Number One singles: Can't Buy Me Love • Eight Days a Week • Get Back • A Hard Day's Night • Hey Jude • Love Me Do • Ticket to Ride • We Can Work It Out • Yellow Submarine • Yesterday • and more.
00306411 Piano/Vocal/Guitar $22.99

Selections from The Beatles Anthology
Volume 1
Free As a Bird and 26 more classics: From Me to You • A Hard Day's Night • Hello Little Girl • Love Me Do • Money • Please Please Me • She Loves You • Twist and Shout • You Really Got a Hold on Me • and more.
00306076 Piano/Vocal/Guitar $19.99

Volume 2
Hello, Goodbye • Help! • I Am the Walrus • Lady Madonna • Lucy in the Sky with Diamonds • Norwegian Wood • Penny Lane • Real Love • Strawberry Fields Forever • Ticket to Ride • and more.
00306103 Piano/Vocal/Guitar $17.95

Volume 3
All Things Must Pass • Blackbird • Cry Baby Cry • The End • Hey Jude • I'm So Tired • Junk • Let It Be • Piggies • Why Don't We Do It in the Road • and more.
00306144 Piano/Vocal/Guitar $17.95

The Beatles – The Capitol Albums
Volume 1
Volume 1 features 42 songs from The Beatles' original Capitol recordings: All My Loving • And I Love Her • I Saw Her Standing There • I Want to Hold Your Hand • If I Fell • She Loves You • You Can't Do That • and dozens more.
00306840 Piano/Vocal/Guitar $19.95

Volume 2
45 more songs from the Capitol collections, including: Hard Day's Night • Do You Want to Know a Secret? • Eight Days a Week • Help! • I've Just Seen a Face • Michelle • Norwegian Wood • Please Please Me • Ticket to Ride • Twist and Shout • and more.
00306841 Piano/Vocal/Guitar $19.95

The Beatles – 1962-1966
26 of their greatest early hits: And I Love Her • Day Tripper • Eight Days a Week • I Want to Hold Your Hand • Love Me Do • Yellow Submarine • Yesterday • more.
00306373 Piano/Vocal/Guitar $19.95

The Beatles – 1967-1970
28 more classics: All You Need Is Love • The Ballad of John and Yoko • Hey Jude • Penny Lane • Revolution • Strawberry Fields Forever • and more.
00306374 Piano/Vocal/Guitar $22.99

Beatles Ballads – 2nd Edition
32 songs, including: And I Love Her • Blackbird • Here, There and Everywhere • Let It Be • Norwegian Wood (This Bird Has Flown) • Yesterday • and more.
00308236 Piano/Vocal/Guitar $16.99

Beatles Best – 2nd Edition
More than 120 Beatles hits: All My Loving • And I Love Her • Come Together • Eleanor Rigby • Get Back • Help! • Hey Jude • I Want to Hold Your Hand • Let It Be • Michelle • many, many more.
00356223 Piano/Vocal/Guitar $34.99

The Beatles – Live at the Hollywood Bowl
16 songs from the 2016 album release: All My Loving • Baby's in Black • Boys • Can't Buy Me Love • Dizzy Miss Lizzie • Everybody's Trying to Be My Baby • A Hard Day's Night • Help! • I Want to Hold Your Hand • Long Tall Sally • She Loves You • She's a Woman • Things We Said Today • Ticket to Ride • Twist and Shout • You Can't Do That.
00202247 Piano/Vocal/Guitar $16.99

Love Songs of the Beatles – 2nd Edition
This second edition has been revised to include 25 favorite love songs from the Fab Four, including: All My Loving • All You Need Is Love • And I Love Her • Eight Days a Week • From Me to You • Girl • Here, There and Everywhere • Hey Jude • I Want to Hold Your Hand • In My Life • Love Me Do • Michelle • Something • Yesterday • and more.
00356224 Piano/Vocal/Guitar $14.99

The Beatles Sheet Music Collection
440 pages featuring over 100 timeless hits, including: All My Loving • Blackbird • Can't Buy Me Love • Don't Let Me Down • Eight Days a Week • Eleanor Rigby • Here Comes the Sun • Hey Jude • I Want to Hold Your Hand • In My Life • Let It Be • Norwegian Wood (This Bird Has Flown) • Ob-La-Di, Ob-La-Da • Penny Lane • Revolution • Twist and Shout • When I'm Sixty-Four • Yesterday • and more.
00236171 Piano/Vocal/Guitar $34.99

The Beatles – Abbey Road
All 17 songs from the classic album: Carry That Weight • Come Together • Golden Slumbers • Here Comes the Sun • Maxwell's Silver Hammer • Something • and more.
00295914 Piano/Vocal/Guitar $16.99

The Beatles – Revolver
All 14 tracks from the 1966 Beatles album that includes classic hits like: Eleanor Rigby • Good Day Sunshine • Got to Get You into My Life • Here, There and Everywhere • I Want to Tell You • Taxman • Yellow Submarine • and more!
00295911 Piano/Vocal/Guitar $16.99

The Beatles – Sgt. Pepper's Lonely Hearts Club Band
Matching folio to classic album. 12 songs, including: With a Little Help from My Friends • Lucy in the Sky with Diamonds • When I'm Sixty Four • A Day in the Life.
00358168 Piano/Vocal/Guitar $16.99

The Beatles – Yellow Submarine/The White Album
30 songs from these albums: All You Need Is Love • Back in the USSR • Birthday • Blackbird • Ob-La-Di, Ob-La-Da • Revolution • While My Guitar Gently Weeps • Yellow Submarine • many more.
00356236 Piano/Vocal/Guitar $19.95

The Beatles – Yellow Submarine
15 classic songs, including: All Together Now • Eleanor Rigby • Lucy in the Sky with Diamonds • Sgt. Pepper's Lonely Hearts Club Band • When I'm Sixty-Four • With a Little Help from My Friends • Yellow Submarine • & more.
00313146 Piano/Vocal/Guitar $16.99

Beatlemania
1967-1970 (Volume 2)
45 of the Beatles biggest hits from 1967-1970, including: All You Need Is Love • Come Together • Hey Jude • Let It Be • The Long and Winding Road • Penny Lane • Revolution • many more!
00356222 Piano/Vocal/Guitar $19.95